The Country Contributor:

The Life and Times

of

Juliet V. Strauss

Ray E. Boomhower

Guild Press of Indiana, Inc.
Carmel, IN

ISBN:1-57860-064-2

Library of Congress Catalog Card No.: 98-72782

This one is for my Mother and Father

"Housekeeping ain't no joke."

The cook Hannah in Louisa May Alcott's *Little Women* (1868)

Preface

In her book *Biography: The Craft and the Calling*, Catherine Drinker Bowen, who in her eclectic career examined the lives of such figures as Tchaikovsky, Oliver Wendell Holmes Jr., John Adams, and Francis Bacon, states that the biographer's aim is to "bring to life, persons and times long vanished. He [the biographer] has a conception of his hero which he desires to share; he cannot bear that this man should be forgotten or exist only in dry eulogy or brief paragraphs of the history textbooks."[1] David McCullough, author of best-selling biographies of Theodore Roosevelt and Harry S. Truman and a Bowen admirer, agrees with her assessment, but adds that a biographer "must genuinely care about his subject."[2]

Both of these writers offer sound advice for the budding biographer. It is advice that I took to heart in my work detailing the life and times of "The Country Contributor," Juliet V. Strauss of Rockville, Indiana. I first came across Strauss while doing research for an article on Indiana's centennial celebration for *Traces of Indiana and Midwestern History* in 1991. Her life and work intrigued me and I subsequently wrote an article about her career for the spring 1995 issue of *Traces*, which examined Hoosier literature. Through the years, I have developed a genuine fondness for this Hoosier original whose column "The Ideas of a Plain Country Woman" in the *Ladies' Home Journal* attracted readers from throughout the country. It was not only her work for the *Ladies' Home Journal*, and her columns in both the *Rockville Tribune* and *Indianapolis News*, that drew me into investigating her life, but also her dedicated efforts at saving from destruction the scenic splendor that now is Turkey Run State Park.

What writer could resist examining the life of a person who had so dedicated a following that the Woman's Press Club of Indiana spearheaded an effort to erect a statue in Strauss's honor at the park, which was sculpted by Myra R. Richards of Indianapolis. What was it about "The Country Contributor" that inspired this intriguing work, titled *Subjugation?* The impressive statue features a graceful figure of a woman with one arm outstretched holding aloft a slender goblet. Her other hand rests on the head of a peacock, which symbolizes pride. Crouched before the woman are a lion, representing brute force, and a tiger, signifying treachery. In the folds of the gown that fall from her figure are an ape, representing imitation in contrast to the genuine, and a wild boar, signifying gluttony. How many hikers have passed by this site and wondered how it came to be at Turkey Run? This biography answers those questions.

There are, however, more complex reasons for a biographer to devote time and energy to his or her craft. I would be remiss if I failed to point out that I was drawn to Strauss in part because she captivated me with her frank comments about her life and career. In one example, she wrote George Cottman, Hoosier historian and *Indiana Magazine of History* founder, expressing her frustration early in her career over her failed attempts at convincing publishers to print her work. She confessed to Cottman that it made her "sick to see others who have scarcely a grain of talent printing their trash in respectable publications."[3] A bitter and self-serving statement perhaps, but it is also an honest one. I would be remiss, too, if I did not mention that writing and obtaining publication of the book will gain for me some small measure of immortality. I can identify with Cottman, who, upon starting his magazine, admitted that part of what drew him into such a venture was not only that it might "edify all who partook of its quarterly doses," but also that it would "perpetuate the memory of myself, who otherwise was in danger of getting lost in time's shuffle."[4] Like Cottman, I hope to avoid such a fate. With this work, I hope, too, to resurrect Strauss's life from history's dustbin.

Except for the chapter detailing Strauss's work to save Turkey Run from the woodsman's axe, chapter titles for this book are taken from ones used in The Country Contributor's book *The Ideas of a Plain Country Woman*, issued by Doubleday, Page & Company in 1908.

Researching and writing a biography is just a portion of the process that results in the publication of a book. There are always a number of people behind the scenes who contribute in a number of ways to make such a project a success. I am particularly indebted to two of Juliet Strauss's great-great-grandchildren, Cynthia Snowden and Andrew Snowden, who provided photographs and other materials on their relative's life.

Lending invaluable assistance and advice on the manuscript were three fine editors, Paula Corpuz, Indiana Historical Society senior editor, Megan McKee, IHS editor (who also happens to be my wife), and Kathy Breen, IHS assistant editor. All three gave up their personal time to lend their editorial skills to the book. Of course, any errors or omissions in the book are mine and mine alone.

I would also like to thank the staffs at the IHS's William Henry Smith Memorial Library, the Indiana State Library's Indiana Division, and Lilly Library at Indiana University for their help in securing the documents, photographs, and other materials needed for researching and publishing this book. My particular gratitude to Susan Sutton, IHS visual collections coordinator, and Steve Towne of the Commission on Public Records, Indiana State Archives, for their assistance with this project.

And, last but not least, my heartfelt thanks to Nancy Baxter at Guild Press of Indiana for publishing the book and the enthusiasm she displayed for the project.

Notes

[1] Catherine Drinker Bowen, *Biography: The Craft and the Calling* (Boston: Little, Brown, 1969), 48–49.

[2] David McCullough, "The Unexpected Harry Truman," in William Zinsser, editor, *Extraordinary Lives: The Art and Craft of American Biography* (Boston: Houghton Mifflin, 1986), 33.

[3] Juliet V. Strauss to George Cottman, 4 March 1897, Cottman Papers, Indiana State Library, Indianapolis.

[4] George S. Cottman, "The Indiana Magazine of History: A Retrospect," *Indiana Magazine of History* 25 (December 1929): 283.

Chronology

1863	Born in Rockville, Indiana, to William and Susan Humphries (January 7)
1867	William Humphries dies (December 27)
1880	First article, "At the Rink," appears in *Rockville Tribune* (March 18)
1880	Juliet Humphries marries Isaac Strouse, changes name to Juliet Strauss (December 22)
1882	Strouse becomes partner with John H. Beadle in *Rockville Tribune*
1883	Daughter Marcia Frances born (June 20)
1887	Daughter Sarah Katherine born (January 3)
1889	Strouse takes over as sole owner and editor of *Rockville Tribune* (October)
1893	"Squibs and Sayings" column first appears in *Rockville Tribune* (February 9)
1903	Susan Humphries dies (January 7)
1903	"Country Contributor" column begins in *Indianapolis News* (November 21)
1905	"Ideas of a Plain Country Woman" column begins in *Ladies' Home Journal* (November)
1908	Book featuring her *Journal* columns published as *The Ideas of a Plain Country Woman*, released by Doubleday, Page & Company of New York
1912	Daughter Sarah Katherine dies (April 28)
1915	Writes letter to Indiana governor Samuel Ralston urging action to save Turkey Run (April 19)
1915	Ralston appoints Strauss, William Woollen, and Vida Newsom to Turkey Run Commission (April 27)

1916   Ralston adds Richard Lieber to Turkey Run Commission (January)

1916   Indiana Historical Commission creates State Park Memorial Committee, which includes Turkey Run Commission, to help create state park system as part of state centennial celebration. Lieber appointed committee chairman (January)

1916   Turkey Run sold at auction for $30,200 to Hoosier Veneer Company of Indianapolis (May 18)

1916   Hoosier Veneer Company agrees to sell Turkey Run to park committee (November 11)

1918   Strauss dies at her home, "Grouch Place," in Rockville (May 22)

1922   *Subjugation* statue by Myra Richards dedicated to Strauss at Turkey Run State Park (July)

1934   Strouse dies in Rockville (December 5)

1974   Marcia Strouse Ott, the couple's daughter and *Rockville Republican* columnist, dies at Hoosier Village, Indianapolis

INTRODUCTION

Indiana's Turkey Run State Park, located in Marshall, Parke County, has within its 2,382 acres some of the Hoosier state's finest scenery. Richard Lieber, noted environmentalist and the first director of the Indiana Department of Conservation, described the area as "a paradise of rocky gorges, glens, bathing beaches and waterfalls, a retreat for song birds, and a garden of wild flowers."[1] Each year thousands of visitors hike through the park's thirteen miles of trails, marveling at such natural features as Rocky Hollow, Gypsy Gulch, Wedge Rock, Turkey Run Hollow, and Devil's Ice Box. On 18 May 1916, however, most of the land that now makes up Turkey Run, also known as Bloomingdale Glens, seemed under threat. For years the land, which had been originally settled in 1826 by Captain Salmon Lusk and passed on to his son, John, had been open for Hoosiers to visit and enjoy. The Indianapolis, Decatur & Springfield Railroad had even opened a resort to house the steady stream of visitors to the area. After John Lusk died in 1915, however, his heirs planned to auction off the land. A park committee of the Indiana Historical Commission (created by the state legislature to commemorate the nineteenth state's centennial) made a valiant effort to buy the land and save it for future generations to enjoy, but the Hoosier Veneer Company of Indianapolis outbid the committee by the slim margin of $100, purchasing the property at auction for $30,200. The firm intended to cut down a vast number of magnificent beech, walnut, oak, sycamore, maple, and poplar trees that dotted the landscape.

On assignment covering the auction for the *Indianapolis News* that day was its ace reporter William Herschell, later better known to Hoosiers as author of the 1919 celebratory poem "Ain't God Good to Indiana?" To Herschell, who had been one of more than two thou-

sand people that attended the auction, it seemed as though Turkey
Run had "passed into the hands of those who, for the dollars of today, would wreck a State's happiness tomorrow." Walking along a path
skirting Sugar Creek, which meanders its way through the area, and
reflecting on the day's events, the reporter met by chance a member
of the delegation brought by the park committee to save the land from
the woodsman's axe—a local woman who had often played in Turkey Run's woods as a child, whose own children had followed in her
footsteps, and who had been among the first to call for the area to be
conserved. "I am sick of soul," the tear-stained woman told Herschell.
"Who would have dreamed that a few men's dollars could step in and
destroy all this, the most beautiful spot in all Indiana, one that all
the money in the world could not restore once it is gone."[2]

Herschell realized that the woman's tears were not those of resignation at a lost cause, but rather "fighting tears, the kind that the
bravest warrior sheds when he is going into battle."[3] The journalist's
assessment proved to be true; the fight to save Turkey Run from destruction was far from over. Six months after the initial auction, the
park committee—bolstered by financial contributions from the public
and the owners of the Indianapolis Motor Speedway—finally reached
a settlement with the Indianapolis timber company, which accepted
a $40,200 offer for the site. Eventually, Turkey Run became Indiana's
second-ever state park (McCormick's Creek in Owen County had
earned the honor of being the first state park while negotiations over
Turkey Run were still going on.)

The tears that had so moved Herschell, a veteran reporter, had
come from Juliet Virginia Strauss, well-known to the citizens of her
hometown, Rockville, Indiana, and to readers nationwide under her
nom de plume, "The Country Contributor." This homemaker who
struggled so hard to save the forests of her youth wrote a steady stream
of common-sense, down-to-earth observations on life for Indiana
readers of her weekly "Country Contributor" column in the *Indianapolis News* and for the approximately one million *Ladies' Home
Journal* women who read her column "The Ideas of a Plain Country

Woman." Edward Bok, the Dutch immigrant who built the *Journal* into a mainstay in American middle-class homes during the early twentieth century, had no hesitation in saying that Strauss's contributions "have been more widely read and . . . are more popular than the writings of any single contributor to the magazine." Her popularity, he added, came because she touched "upon the vital wellsprings of living with a hand that we feel is that of experience."[4] Strauss's writing found—in addition to frequent hardships and struggles—joy, beauty, and art in a homemaker's daily life. "I know what it is to be poor and to be held down seemingly to a level beneath my natural abilities," Strauss wrote. "I know what it means to be tired of the dishrag and sick of the coal-scuttle, but I have learned . . . that there is a way of accepting these things which lift them to the level of the brush and the pen and the strings of the harp or the violin."[5]

Her writing, emphasizing the true worth of being a dedicated homemaker, followed in the footsteps of earlier writers like Catharine E. Beecher who, in such works as *A Treatise on Domestic Economy, for the Use of Young Ladies at Home and at School* (1841) and *The American Woman's Home* (1869), attempted to elevate "both the honor and the remuneration of all employments that sustain the many difficult and varied duties of the family state, and thus to render each department of woman's profession as much desired and respected as are the most honored professions of men."[6] Strauss's efforts to glorify homemaking struck a chord with her female readers across the country who grew, through long association, to consider the Rockville housewife "as friend and counselor," the *Indianapolis News* commented upon Strauss's death on 22 May 1918. She offered through her essays, the newspaper noted, a sound philosophy: "a love of simplicity and genuineness, an earnest and honest faith, a hatred of sham and pretense, and a belief in the home and family as the great educators."[7]

Bok's high praise for Strauss's contributions might have been prompted by her willingness to follow the dictates of the *Journal's* editorial philosophy that a woman's proper place consisted of being in the home serving the needs of her husband and children.[8] This attitude stood in stark contrast to the emergence of the college educated, sometimes unmarried, and self-supporting "New Women" of the 1890s, who, like Jane Addams of Hull House fame, as historian Nancy Woloch notes, "integrated Victorian virtues with an activist social role."[9] More and more American women during the late nineteenth and early twentieth centuries were finding opportunities for fulfillment outside the home—joining the labor force in large numbers (the number of working women in Indiana grew from 116,716 in 1900 to 185,385 ten years later), fighting for social reforms like temperance, broadening their intellectual horizons through membership in women's clubs, and agitating for equality with men, especially the right to vote.[10] But Strauss, who prided herself "on plain living and high thinking," advocated in her work a strictly traditional role for females of home and hearth.[11] "I wish I could shake them [women] awake," Strauss wrote, "to the importance of little daily affairs that have to do with the bodily life—the clear fire, the good dinner, the simple house-keeping and home-keeping that is woman's best estate."[12]

In one of her pieces for the *Journal* (later reprinted in her only book *The Ideas of a Plain Country Woman*), titled "The Woman Who Wears the Halo," she called the woman's movement "a delusion" and claimed that "most of the aspirations that women are struggling with are fool notions promulgated by somebody who hasn't anything better to do." Women attain their highest glory through the "simple carrying out of a manifest destiny, a brave and cheerful acceptance of the existing order of things." She goes on to say:

> The intelligent woman who has done real work—and by real work I mean labour with her own hands year after year in her own house and kitchen—and who has meanwhile reared a creditable family and still kept for her soul a pair of wings like a dove, is the perfect flower of civilisation, far superior to the woman of the world who knows the lingo of polite society and little else.

The people who count in this world are those who, if everybody were suddenly stripped of every worldly possession, cast upon a desert shore, and confronted with only the raw material for living, would know how to take hold of it.[13]

Strauss's fulminations against such figures as the "man woman, the woman athlete, the bachelor maid, the 'bohemian' literary woman with 'advanced views'" and, especially, the "supremacy of the perfectly groomed and well-mannered lady," were formed not out of any political convictions on her part (she claimed to be not anti-suffrage, or anti-anything), but on her personal experiences growing up in Rockville.[14] During her early childhood her family, who had roots in the South, was excommunicated from the Presbyterian church for supposedly being Confederate sympathizers during the Civil War. Following her father's death, Strauss and her family had been looked down upon for their poverty by the upper ranks of Rockville society. Pretty, poor, talented, and fatherless girls, noted Strauss, always made a "fine target for village gossips and for the slings and arrows of outrageous fortune as dealt out by more fortunate girls who have fathers and big brothers and money and 'social position.'"[15] Unsurprisingly, Strauss titled an autobiographical series of articles in the *Ladies' Home Journal* about her early life "The Chronicles of a Queer Girl." Married at a young age to a young Jewish man from the "wrong side of the tracks," she and her husband, who struggled to earn a living as operators of a small-town newspaper, were excluded from the literary and other social clubs that sprang up in the community at the turn of the century. "I ought to be chairman of a General Committee on Social Unpopularity," Strauss once said. "I was born under a social ban, and my whole life has been spent on the shady side of social life."[16] Although she claimed that these experiences did not embitter her, Strauss did emphasize in her writings the overwhelming importance of a woman finding her place at home, and the dignity and worth of such an existence over the fashionable and elegant lives lived by society ladies. "Being a plain home woman," she argued, "is one of the greatest successes in life, if to plainness you add kindness, tolerance, and interest, real interest in simple things."[17]

Real life was not in the social whirl of clubs and receptions, Strauss wrote, but instead "in the kitchen where the woman must, with consummate cleverness, never be excelled by an art of accomplishment, minister to the bodily wants of a few of her fellow-creatures." The woman who walked across fields on a winter evening to help a fellow female in a moment of need, one who dressed a newborn baby or prepared a body for burial, harnessed horses, milked cows, saved young lambs from perishing in rough weather—it is she, not the "perfectly groomed and well-mannered lady," who has seen life, Strauss said. She boldly dared any woman's rights supporter to say that in her career of making speeches and meeting men on terms of equality "she has found anything better than a good man's love, or that there is any state of affairs, or domestic arrangements that exceeds the happiness of a comfortable home with father, mother, and children."[18]

Strauss's traditional views on the place of women in American society—she stated that if a home was not an essential part of a woman's life "there is something wrong with her"—found acceptance with both female and male readers across the nation.[19] During her career Strauss came to be considered as one of the most widely read female writers in America. Indiana historian Jacob Piatt Dunn Jr., who noted that Strauss's writing possessed the Hoosier characteristic of "optimism and wholesomeness," claimed that the Rockville writer was "more widely read than any American essayist has ever been, not even excepting Emerson." In the history of the world, Dunn went on to say of Strauss, "nobody ever wrote so much about the common things of everyday life, and held their readers."[20] Strauss nevertheless struggled early in her married life to reconcile her yearning for success with her equally strong desire to be a devoted wife and mother. "I have been blessed with the knowledge," she once stated, "that cooking a dinner for one's own family is as honorable and satisfactory as writing a bright article."[21] But in her private correspondence with other Hoosier authors during the state's golden age of literature in the late nineteenth and early twentieth centuries, Strauss revealed her frustrations at having inadequate time, because of her domestic chores, to dedicate to her budding literary career. "I have so very many cares and so much hard work to do," she protested, "that I can find little time for writing."

Considering herself "ill starred" as far as having any luck in getting her early work, including poetry and short stories, published, she noted that it made her "sick to see others who have scarcely a grain of talent printing their trash in respectable publications."[22] Strauss longed to have more than the success she enjoyed with her newspaper work, which along with her writing in the *Indianapolis News* included her weekly "Squibs and Sayings" column that appeared in her hometown newspaper, the *Rockville Tribune*, owned and operated by her husband, Isaac R. Strouse. Instead of the seemingly endless grind of churning out copy for newspapers, a task she grew to detest early in her career, Strauss wanted to use her time to write short stories and poems that might receive the same national acclaim as that enjoyed by such Hoosier writers as James Whitcomb Riley (a Strauss friend and confidant), Booth Tarkington, Meredith Nicholson, Charles Majors, Maurice Thompson, Gene Stratton-Porter, and others. The success achieved by these authors fueled the ambitions of Strauss and other would-be Hoosier writers. This was a time in Indiana when "it was difficult to forecast who would next turn poet," Nicholson noted. Indianapolis journalist Charles Dennis noted that the fever for poetry got so bad that there appeared in his community "a peculiar crooking of the right elbow and furtive sliding of the hand into the pocket, which was an unfailing preliminary to the reading of a poem."[23]

Strauss, who peppered her "Squibs and Sayings" column with her poetry and also contributed a number of poems to Indianapolis newspapers, poured out her frustrations at her situation in life in her poem "Hidden Fires," which was published in the 1900 book *A Representative Collection of the Poetry of Indiana during the First Hundred Years of Its History as Territory and State.* She wrote:

So strong within my bosom burned
The sacred flame of poesy,
Cold, world-wise faces from me turned,
Though some looked back and pitied me!
So, then, lest men should see that flame
Alight on lip and cheek and eye,
I banked my fires, and covered them
Because I could not let them die.

Then eagerly I sought for those
Whose hearts burned incense like my own,
For friends to whom I might disclose
The altar where my offering shone.

I could not bear to live and die
From human fellowship apart;
But while I sought society,
The hidden flames consumed my heart.

Now, since this rare poetic age
Has dawned, men seek the hidden shrine
Wherein there glowed in other days
The fervor of that flame divine,

And cry, "Show us what men did spurn!"
I make some smiling, light reply—
Lest they should glimpse the burned-out urn
Wherein a few white ashes lie![24]

Her home life too, offered numerous challenges for Strauss. Her husband, Isaac Strouse, whom she described as a "Tom Sawyer village lad," offered little or no help in raising the couple's two daughters, Marcia Frances and Sarah Katherine (whose death at age twenty-five hit Strauss very hard). Strauss categorized men into two distinct types: domestic, a man who will "go to church with his wife, and set the hens, and run the clothes through the wringer, and read aloud from the farm paper while she [his wife] fashions garments for the little ones from the worn-out raiment of their elders;" and the other kind. Her husband was the other kind. "He [Strouse] was a sportsman, a man of the streets and town," said Strauss, "a man's man in every sense of the word—and I was a mother, a child in years, but I had a world to make for my children, a castle to build—and how was I to build it unless I learned to make bricks without straw?"[25] The hard work she had to endure as a housewife may have prompted Strauss's rueful reflection later in life that husbands were "all right I guess, if you have to go somewhere and all the other women have them."[26]

There were those who appreciated Strauss's talents and supported her literary endeavors. John H. Beadle, *Rockville Tribune* owner and later roving correspondent for the American Press Association, was the first to print Strauss's writings and advised her mother that her daughter possessed literary skills and should be encouraged to write. John Clark Ridpath, educator and a best-selling popular historian, was an early admirer of her writing. Thomas Rice, lawyer and United States diplomat, commended her writing before her fellow Rockville citizens. George S. Cottman gave the Rockville writer advice on her fiction and urged her to become more active in literary organizations like the Western Association of Writers. Later in life, when she had won national attention through her column in the *Ladies' Home Journal*, the Hoosier Poet himself, James Whitcomb Riley, kept up a lively correspondence with Strauss that featured praise for her writing and concern for her health.

Few of Strauss's writings survive today, except in newspaper morgues and on microfilm. She produced only one book, *The Ideas of a Plain Country Woman*, a collection of her columns and some new essays, and her often flowery, prosaic writing style long ago fell out of fashion. The homespun advice she dispensed for her loyal readership typified the themes used by many of the state's leading authors during its literary heyday—a message that idealized traditional values and offered release for readers from a world that seemed to be changing on a daily basis under assault from such forces as industrialization and urbanization. The traditional values, simple pleasures, and nostalgia for a rural life emphasized by these "Indiana romancers" who wrote so uncritically of life in the Midwest, proved to be less attractive to a post-World War I society preoccupied with business prosperity and such technological marvels as the automobile, radio, and motion pictures.[27]

The women who eagerly read Strauss's writing during her lifetime cared little about their friend's literary shortcomings. Turn-of-the-century homemakers knew that like themselves, Strauss had endured the same struggles they experienced in keeping the family unit whole against sometimes overwhelming odds. There may have been some labor-saving devices on the market, but most homemakers still had to carry in water on a daily basis from wells and pumps for cooking, cleaning, and washing. Just doing a load of laundry—called by one housewife "the great domestic dread of the household"—involved backbreaking work as the homemaker had to heat water on a wood-burning stove and scrub clothes by hand on a washboard using harsh, homemade lye soap.[28] Once the clothes were dry, having been hung on clotheslines outdoors, housewives had to use heavy metal irons, known as "sad irons," that were heated on stoves in stifling hot kitchens to finish the job. Most chores performed on a daily basis by homemakers in Indiana, and across the country, at the turn of the century "involved lifting, carrying, digging, pumping or pouring—all using energy and muscle."[29]

Her readers recognized Strauss as one of their own. Homemakers continually turned to her for the homespun advice and encouragement she offered and mourned her passing with poems and letters praising her work printed in newspapers throughout the state. Writing an appreciation about Strauss in the *Indianapolis News* following The Country Contributor's death, Lilian Habich Lennox noted that in her writing Strauss had pointed the way for people, particularly the women of Indiana, to "a broader conception, to a fuller appreciation of life. She made it her concern to hold up for reverence the household drudge, that uncomplaining burden-bearer who, she insisted, was behind the smooth-running mechanism of each home."[30] In 1922 the Woman's Press Club of Indiana erected a more concrete tribute to Strauss, dedicating a statue titled *Subjugation* in her memory at Turkey Run. Sculpted by Myra R. Richards of Indianapolis, the monument, the Press Club claimed, captured the true spirit of Strauss's writing—the subjugation of the material to the spiritual. The work also honored the Rockville native's role in saving the lush forests of her youth from destruction. "We were all so grateful that Turkey Run had been saved from the timber interests," said Susan McWhirter Ostrom, Woman's Press Club recording secretary, "and felt Mrs. Strauss should be memorialized for her leadership in creating public sentiment for this state park to be saved."[31]

Whatever the critical response—positive or negative—to her work, Strauss refused to offer any apologies for the path she chose for herself. "There are not theories in my curriculum," she said. "I only know a little, and that little I learned by living." Strauss said she did not like writing about herself nor did she try to make herself a heroine. "It is only that I desire to share with the poor and the struggling," she claimed, "what I learned by being born into the ranks of the poor and struggling."[32] Looking back on her life after her children had grown up and moved away from home, Strauss expressed pride at never following anyone's lead. "I lived my own life," she proudly stated. "If I wished to ride a horse, or to play a game of cards, or to go wading in the creek with the children, I always did it. I never strained my eyesight or racked my nerves trying to arrive at small perfections. I avoided rivalries and emulations. In short, I lived."[33]

Notes

[1] Harlow Lindley, editor, *The Indiana Centennial, 1916: A Record of the Celebration of the One Hundredth Anniversary of Indiana's Admission to Statehood* (Indianapolis: Indiana Historical Commission, 1919), 50.

[2] The Department of Conservation, State of Indiana, *Turkey Run State Park: A History and Description* (Indianapolis: William B. Burford, Contractor for State Printing and Binding, 1919), 42.

[3] Ibid.

[4] The Country Contributor [Juliet Strauss], *The Ideas of a Plain Country Woman* (New York: Doubleday, Page & Company, 1908), v–vi.

[5] The Country Contributor, "The Ideas of a Plain Country Woman," *Ladies' Home Journal*, July 1907.

[6] Catharine E. Beecher and Harriet Beecher Stowe, *The American Woman's Home or, Principles of Domestic Science; Being a Guide to the Formation and Maintenance of Economical, Healthful, Beautiful and Christian Homes* (1869; reprint, Hartford, Conn.: The Stowe-Day Foundation, 1994), 17. See also, Suellen Hoy, *Chasing Dirt: The American Pursuit of Cleanliness* (New York: Oxford University Press, 1995), 19–23, and Susan Strasser, *Never Done: A History of American Housework* (New York: Pantheon Books, 1982), 185-195.

[7] "Juliet V. Strauss," *Indianapolis News*, 23 May 1918.

[8] Bok protested openly in the *Ladies' Home Journal* about the growth of women's clubs. In an article, "My Quarrel with Women's Clubs," he said that he was not opposed to a woman joining a club, provided she "join merely one, and does not place its interest, in importance, before the higher duties of the home." The average club for women, he went on to say, had done "incalculable harm" to women by a developing a type of female with only "woman's-club knowledge" that was actually an "undigested, superficial knowledge that is worse than no knowledge at all, since what she knows she knows wrong." See Edward Bok, "My Quarrel with Women's Clubs," *Ladies' Home Journal*, January 1910.

[9] Nancy Woloch, *Women and the American Experience* (New York: McGraw-Hill, Inc., 1994), 269–71. See also, Sarah M. Evans, *Born for Lib-*

erty: A History of Women in America (New York: The Free Press, 1989), 147–8, and Dorothy and Carl J. Schneider, *American Women in the Progressive Era, 1900–1920* (1993; reprint, New York: Anchor Books, 1994), 16–18.

[10] For women in Indiana labor, see Clifton J. Phillips, *Indiana in Transition: The Emergence of an Industrial Commonwealth, 1880–1920* (Indianapolis: Indiana Historical Bureau and Indiana Historical Society, 1968), 327–31. For social reform movements like women's suffrage and temperance in the state, see Phillips, *Indiana in Transition*, 494–502; Justin E. Walsh, *The Centennial History of the Indiana General Assembly, 1816–1978* (Indianapolis: The Select Committee on the Centennial History of the Indiana General Assembly, in cooperation with the Indiana Historical Bureau, 1978), 168–71; and James H. Madison, *The Indiana Way: A State History* (Bloomington and Indianapolis: Indiana University Press and Indiana Historical Society, 1986), 224–26. For the national picture, see Schneider, *American Women in the Progressive Era*, 95–100, 103–6.

[11] The Country Contributor, "Ideas of a Plain Country Woman," *Ladies' Home Journal*, June 1912.

[12] Strauss, *The Ideas of a Plain Country Woman*, 9.

[13] Ibid., 10–27.

[14] Ibid., 5–6.

[15] The Country Contributor, "Ideas of a Plain Country Woman," *Ladies' Home Journal*, October 1907.

[16] The Country Contributor, "The Ideas of a Plain Country Woman," *Ladies' Home Journal*, June 1910.

[17] Strauss, *The Ideas of a Plain Country Woman*, 18

[18] Ibid., 62, 156.

[19] Ibid., 115.

[20] Jacob Piatt Dunn Jr., *Indiana and Indianans* 5 Vols. (Chicago: The American Historical Society, 1919), 2:1196–97.

[21] "Talented Writer at Home in Rockville," *Indianapolis News*, 29 August 1903.

[22] Juliet Strauss to George Cottman, 4 March 1897, Cottman Papers, Indiana State Library, Indianapolis.

[23] Meredith Nicholson, *The Hoosiers* (New York: The MacMillan Company, 1916), 27–28.

[24] Compiled edition by Benjamin S. Parker and Enose B. Heiney, A

Representative Collection of the Poetry of Indiana during the First Hundred Years of its History as Territory and State, 1800 to 1900 (New York: Silver Burdett and Company, 1900), 383.

[25] Strauss, *The Ideas of a Plain Country Woman*, 90–91.

[26] Cynthia Snowden to Ray Boomhower, E–mail, 12 February 1997.

[27] Ronald Weber, *The Midwestern Ascendancy in American Writing* (Bloomington and Indianapolis: Indiana University Press, 1992), 3, 15–16. For more on the golden age in Indiana literature, see also Arthur W. Shumaker, *A History of Indiana Literature: With Emphasis on the Authors of Imaginative Works Who Commenced Writing Prior to World War II* (Indianapolis: Indiana Historical Bureau, 1962); Howard H. Peckham, "What Made Hoosiers Write?" *American Heritage* (Autumn 1950); and Phillips, *Indiana in Transition*, 503–25.

[28] Strasser, *Never Done*, 104.

[29] Eleanor Arnold, editor, *Voices of American Homemakers* (Bloomington and Indianapolis: Indiana University Press, 1985), 11. See also, Arnold, editor, *Party Lines, Pumps and Privies: Memories of Hoosier Homemakers* (Indianapolis: Indiana Extension Homemakers Association, 1984); Arnold, editor, *Feeding Our Families: Memories of Hoosier Homemakers* (Indianapolis: Indiana Extension Homemakers Association, 1983); and Hoy, *Chasing Dirt*, 157–59.

[30] Lilian Habich Lennox, "The Country Contributor, An Appreciation," *Indianapolis News*, 25 May 1918.

[31] "Spirit of Strauss Fountain Sought," *Indianapolis News*, 30 August 1974.

[32] Strauss, "The Ideas of a Plain Country Woman," *Ladies' Home Journal*, June 1917.

[33] Strauss, *The Ideas of a Plain Country Woman*, 96–97.

Chapter One
THE CHRONICLES OF A QUEER GIRL

Late in the frigid month of January 1824 three men—General Arthur Patterson, General Joseph Orr, and Colonel Thomas Smith—set out into the rolling, wild countryside of Indiana's then three-year-old Parke County, named in honor of Benjamin Parke, who helped frame the state's constitution and later assisted in the founding of the Indiana Historical Society. The small group was searching for a new site for the county seat. Seeking a central location, the trio visited land near the present-day towns of Judson and Catlin. While investigating these areas, they received an invitation to visit Ray's Tavern, a small village situated where Rockville, Indiana, stands today. On about the first of February, the now exhausted men reached the tavern operated by Andrew Ray. According to a Parke County history written by Rockville native and newspaper editor John H. Beadle, the three officials were "royally entertained—for the times. What personal inducements were offered we cannot guess, but by breakfast time next day this spot was chosen [for the county seat]."[1]

A hint as to the "personal inducements" referred to by Beadle can be gleaned from what happened when the three men responsible for the selection of Ray's Tavern as the proper spot for the county seat and local settlers wrangled over a new name for the community. The officials and residents were busy thrashing out their disagreements when legend has it that a bystander, growing weary of the endless debate, went up to a nearby boulder and loudly proclaimed: "This fellow has been here longer that any of you—name the town after him—name it Rockville." With a name successfully chosen, those gathered for the solemn occasion drained a bottle of whiskey and christened the town by breaking the now empty bottle over the rock.[2]

In its early days as the county seat, Rockville's growth was "disgustingly slow." Beadle noted that one of the community's best business lots was exchanged not for cash, but for a rifle.[3] Up until 1851, the county seat was described as a "straggling village, with no municipal government, no system of public improvements beyond those made by individuals."[4] Rockville's rural character reflected the state's standing, as most Hoosiers in the middle of the nineteenth century lived and worked on farms, with only a small portion of Indiana's residents dwelling in communities of more than 2,500 in population.[5] The copious swamps and stagnant ponds that dotted Parke County's landscape helped breed malaria and other illnesses. A longtime doctor in the area recalled that during Rockville's early history a man was "not a good citizen in those days who did not have the chills and fevers. I have come home from a hard day's work among people afflicted with it only to find my wife and daughter afflicted with it also."[6]

In spite of the hardships associated with living in such wild country, the promise of a fresh start lured settlers from all over the United States. Into this rugged area in 1836 came Captain John (a War of 1812 veteran) and Betsy Woods Humphries (also spelled as Humphreys), who emigrated to Rockville from their former home in Augusta County, Virginia. Of Scotch-Irish ancestry, the Humphries, who had eight children, brought with them a young son, William, who grew up in the Hoosier wilderness and became a skilled carpenter, contractor, and house builder. One of his daughters remembered William Humphries as a "big man, six feet two in height and broad in proportion," with hands roughened and gnarled by hard work.[7] "But he was also a gentleman," she added, "quick to perform little services and show little deferences to the women of the family, and missing no small, sweet courtesy by which life is made so beautiful." His code of honor, she said, included always being "honest among men and tender and kind to all women." The daughter recalled one incident where a woman who had come to Rockville from her home in the East to teach school was on her way to church one Sunday when the wind blew off her veil and carried it into the middle of a muddy street. A crowd of young men ignored her predicament, but William Humphries came along and "in the twinkling of an eye the veil was returned to her—though Father's Sunday boots and new black-and-white-checked trousers were badly damaged."[8] On 29 December 1859 William Humphries married Susan Marcia King from Grandview, Illinois, a woman whose future son-in-law Isaac Strouse described as possessing "wonderful mentality and very wide information, a decided gift for literature . . . a brilliant conversationalist and fine linguist," which were qualities she later shared with her three daughters.[9]

The daughter who did the most with what her mother gave her was born on 7 January 1863 in the family's house on West Ohio Street in Rockville, a structure built by William Humphries. The second of the Humphries' three daughters (a son, William Gamaliel, died when he was four years old), Juliet Virginia Humphries was a self-confessed tomboy who enjoyed climbing trees, turning handsprings, and riding astride a horse instead of the more "ladylike" side-saddle fashion. At first "encumbered" with curly hair, Juliet attempted to emancipate herself from the "trials of girlhood" by cutting off the offending curls, leaving her hair "in jagged scallops that necessitated a trip to the barber."[10]

She loved from an early age to wander through her home county's lush forests. His daughter's wanderlust spirit prompted William Humphries to nickname her his "little gypsy girl" (later shortened to "Gyp"), a sobriquet she kept for the rest of her life. "In childhood and girlhood," said Juliet, "I was never dull—I had a talent for making things happen."[11] The young girl developed a deep affection for the natural wonders her home county afforded her, especially an area known as Bloomingdale Glens, preserved, thanks in part to Juliet's efforts, years later as Turkey Run State Park. "It is beauty, rather than grandeur, which characterizes these glens," Juliet later wrote of the area. "The green gloom of hemlock shaded grottoes; the delicate fringes of maiden hair ferns; the gray-green lacings of beautiful lichens on walls of stone; the sunlit vistas beyond overhanging cliffs; the fairy tinkle of miniature falls in the clear bubbling run—all suggest nature in her most seductive mood.[12]

There existed, she recalled, a less sharp distinction during her childhood between country and city life. This was, after all, a time when "small-town life was America's norm."[13] The Humphries lived "close to life and primitive things," said Juliet, "and Nature was very near to us, and we never went very far from the beginning of things."[14] It was quite common for her and her sisters when starting out to church on Sunday to meet along the way "a ponderous mother hog and some ten or eleven squealing progeny, who resolutely refused to turn out and compelled us to take to the gutter, to the ruination of our cloth gaiters." Every twilight evening, the village cows wandered dutifully home to be milked. "We could hear the swish of the milk in the pail blending with the gentle sounds of the summer night—the call of the whippoorwill in the woods and the talking of the young fellows who had dropped by to see us girls," Juliet said.[15]

The bucolic setting of her youth was tempered by a hard reality: Indiana was at war. During the Civil War, the Hoosier state contributed 197,141 troops to the Union cause, ranking second among northern states in numbers contributed. Of that number, 7,243 were killed in battle, and another 17,785 died from disease.[16] But not every Hoosier supported the war. Settlers whose families came from the South still had strong ties with that region and were sometimes sympathetic to the Confederate cause. Although expressing loyalty to the Union, conservative Democrats expressed strong reservations about the executive powers wielded by the Republican administrations, both President Abraham Lincoln's in Washington, D.C., and Indiana governor Oliver P. Morton's in Indianapolis. Fiercely loyal to the Union, Morton used all his powers, and more, as governor to fight what he saw as treasonous elements in the state. The tensions produced by the war created in the state, according to one historian, a "strong partisan feeling" with many people holding the belief that there was no "middle ground between intense patriotism and active disloyalty; between devotion to the union and sympathy for secession; between 'peace democrat' and a 'hissing copperhead.'"[17]

Parke County experienced particularly stormy times during the war years, with sentiment among its citizens divided between the Union and Confederacy. In recounting those years, Maurice Murphy of Rockville noted that the county furnished approximately 2,000 troops for the North, about one-eighth of its population—a figure he considered substantial for a county "in which a large portion of its inhabitants were actively or passively opposed to the subjugation of the South."[18] Unionists in the county ostracized those who were, to their minds, less than wholehearted in their support of the fight against the Confederates; a fate that befell the Humphries. One of Juliet's earliest memories was of her grandfather's funeral and the "fact that nobody would come to help bury him because he was 'an old rebel.'"[19] Juliet also remembered that town boys who supported the men in blue used to delight in throwing stones and breaking windows out of her father's old carpenter shop. The Humphries clan was kicked out of Rockville's New School Presbyterian Church for being "Southern sympathizers" and only welcomed back after the war ended with a Union victory. The church might have had some cause for its action. Juliet recalled that one Sunday her aunts wore "shuck hats," made from corn shucks, to church "as a token of their allegiance" to the South. "My aunts said that if their cousins had to wear such hats," said Juliet, "they, too, would wear them, so they braided one for each of them and they sat up very fierce and militant above my aunt's smooth, evenly parted red hair, and their cheeks, unpleasantly flushed in the excitement of thus flaunting their colors in the face of a northern congregation."[20] During those troubled times the Humphries also sheltered another "sympathizer," Reverend Samuel H. McNutt, a Presbyterian minister who had been dismissed from the pulpit for his supposed allegiance to the Confederates.[21]

Her family's experience with the church, combined with the fierce arguments she heard on religious matters, led Juliet to the conclusion that "religion was a failure and so struck out to be a law unto myself—boldly laying claim to being an agnostic." Although she later realized that this position may have been "silly, dramatic vanity," she tried to be sincere with herself about religion throughout her life. "I felt that I did not know or actually believe anything whatever about the purposes of God," said Juliet, "or whether there was a God, or whether our existence in the universe meant more to Him than that of the molecule or the louse." Considering herself moral, if not religious, Juliet held the creed throughout her life that it made no difference what one believed, "it is what you do that counts."[22]

The years after the war were also unkind to the Humphries. On 27 December 1867 William Humphries died (Juliet attributed the death to appendicitis), leaving behind a widow and four children, the eldest of which was only six years old. At a young age, Juliet had already learned some hard lessons about life. "I knew that Santa Claus did not come down the chimney," she noted, "and that the stork did not bring little brother, and that everybody one meets is not necessarily a friend."[23] Left on her own at age twenty-eight, Susan Humphries managed—with the help of her mother and sisters—to eke out a living for herself and her children by conducting "her affairs with a shrewdness of which few men would have been capable," her son-in-law Strouse said (words he must have felt constituted high praise in those days before the woman's movement).[24] The family survived, moving in with one of its deceased father's sisters, but young Juliet remembered daily battles by her mother to put food on the table and clothes on her daughters' backs. "There was always," she noted, "some crisis at hand."[25] Calling her mother a "heroine," Juliet said that while she did not always believe in her mother's quiet way of enduring life's misfortunes, she heartily approved of her "method of ignoring privations and of living on a broad intellectual scale among very common, discouraging surroundings."[26]

In order to survive, Susan Humphries became a genius at improvisation. While the well-to-do homes in Rockville might be ringed by iron fences with stylish gates, the Humphries' residence sported only a plain, white picket fence with rickety gate posts. "It was a queer house with bare, white doors and plain gables—a house built with a view to simple necessity," said Juliet, "rather than any attempt at ornamentation."[27] The house had been made by her father, who had a habit of constructing extremely solid houses that could withstand tornadoes and earthquakes, but continually neglected to make them "of any sense convenient." For example, the house contained an attic room that bore the name "Purgatory." The room had been christened with that name by William Humphries because it always looked as if the Devil had just flown through it and flapped his wings. Stored in the room were such treasures, to Juliet's eyes at least, as hoopskirts, a Shaker bonnet, a chest with her mother's wedding gown, a box of letters from Virginia, and a tea chest with pictures of pagodas and princesses in dull green and silver. This room was heated, said Juliet, in a "fashion which must have been original with my father." A pipe from the stove in the parlor below ran straight up through the floor and connected into a chimney sitting precariously on top of the house. "On winter Saturday afternoons," she observed, "Mother used to kindle a little fire in the parlor stove to heat up Purgatory for us to play in, and this mysterious warmth that came from the stove-pipe added a charm to the mystic realm where we built our dolls' houses under the sloping eaves."[28]

Luckily for the Humphries food for the family "just growed" in those days, noted Juliet. "We bought a barrel of sugar and a sack of green coffee—and aside from this there was no grocery bill," she said. "Meat lard, flour, meal, honey, cheese, butter, all sorts of vegetables, chickens, turkeys, ducks, geese, fruit—everything to eat—grew up right around us; the streams were teeming with fish, the woods full of game—the 'eating problem' scarcely entered into our calculations."[29] Also, since this was a time before the widespread use of iceboxes, perishable food items like milk, butter, and eggs were often kept cool by being suspended down into a water well during the hot, muggy Indiana summers. When these items were accidentally, or mischievously, dropped into the water, the Humphries had to run to a neighbor's house to borrow the "grab-hook," a long pole with a hook at the end used to retrieve the lost foodstuffs.

Inside the Humphries' home, a visitor could often find a quilt or carpet being made by hand, that is, if the women and children in the family were not busy making apple butter, weeding the garden, or slaughtering a hog for supper. "The fact was that there were many things we had which were not 'made on purpose,' but which would 'do,'" Juliet observed.[30] As the middle child she also endured the indignity of wearing hand-me-down clothes from her older sister. "The new garments were always purchased for the eldest," she said, "and once in a while my little sister came in for a really new frock, there being nothing to descend to her by ordinary generation; but I must invariably have the made-over garments which sister had out-grown."[31]

Her plain dress as a young girl contributed to her indifference later in life to regular church attendance. It may have been pleasant for people to walk up the church aisle if they possessed "a new hat and coat and a silk petticoat that rustles faintly," Juliet said, but there was little compensation for sitting in the front pew if "your aunt wears her old Paisley shawl forever . . . and when you are in a chronic state of outgrowing your Sunday frock and are fearfully conscious of your white woolen stockings."[32] On many a Sabbath morning Juliet re-membered having "red eyes and broken spirit, over having to wear some skimpy garment made out of such solid spots of material as could be found after the dress had been turned upside down and 'hindside front' to extract every bit of 'wear' possible for its original owner."[33] The lessons in self-sufficiency Juliet learned in her youth, however, stood her in good stead in later life when she struggled to raise a family on her husband's meager income as editor of a small-town weekly newspaper.

The Humphries may have wanted for material possessions, but they were rich in other areas. "We were poor only in wordly goods and gear," said Juliet. "Our spiritual and intellectual endowment was very fair. There is no poverty like narrowness of mind and soul, but we had treasures that moth and rust could not corrupt. Poetry, history, books of travel and romance made bright the hours of winter evenings. Discussions of questions in philosophy, theology, and national politics hastened the hours of toil. We were not unhappy people."[34] One of the keys to the family's happiness was that Susan Humphries constantly endeavored to instill in her daughters such refining influences as reading, an activity Juliet remembered as being frowned upon as extravagant by their neighbors. A person could hardly turn around in the Humphries' kitchen without discovering a copy of an entertaining and instructive book. Family favorites included works by such English authors as Charles Dickens and William Makepeace Thackeray as well as stories from *The Arabian Nights*. "My mother was an unfailing judge of literature," noted Juliet.[35]

There existed, however, some reading material that Susan Humphries attempted to keep out of reach of her daughter's eager hands. Juliet recalled once when her mother locked away in a top bureau drawer Charlotte Bontë's novel *Jane Eyre*. But in one instance the mother's efforts to safeguard her progeny from "improper" reading material failed. Her mother had caught Juliet reading potboiler stories featured in the *New York Ledger*, a newspaper in which one of her uncles had a subscription, a discovery that caused Susan Humphries to bar the periodical from her home. "I was so disconsolate over this decree," said Juliet, "that uncle, who was fatally 'goodhearted,' took to hiding the papers in a cunning little hole in the haymow where I could find them and read the beloved stories when mother thought I was at play." Her mother eventually caught on to the ruse being perpetrated on her, but relented and allowed her daughter to read the newspaper in the house.[36]

In addition to a love for literature, Susan Humphries attempted to instill in her daughters an appreciation for music. Some of Juliet's favorite early memories involved her aunts and one uncle, who sounded to the youngster like "bumblebees in a clover-field on a summer day," sitting around the fireplace singing such old favorites as "Loving Kindness" and "Our Bondage Here Shall End." The

Humphries also owned a piano and Juliet loved to hear her sister Betty play the compositions of such composers as Mendelssohn and "dearly loved the atmosphere of music about the house." Although Juliet claimed that her "accomplishments as a musician amounted to nothing," later in life she impressed her daughter Marcia with her ability at the piano and her constant singing as she "worked, or rocked my little sister, or as we sat by her in the twilight."[37]

From an early age, Juliet and her sisters were often warned by their mother and aunts never to "sink down" by associating with those whom they considered the lower class of society. Whenever one of the Humphries' girls was seen accompanying members of this group, an aunt expressed her contempt by asking the offending party what she meant by "colloguin' with such people?" Juliet confessed that she was an inveterate "collogeur" because she enjoyed meeting "interesting people and I was always picking up some friend from the mammon of unrighteousness."[38] Juliet and her sisters also failed to display the proper respectful attitude when it came to entertaining guests at their home. In spite of warnings of punishments that would be meted out if they misbehaved by laughing or speaking at the table, they often did just that, leaving the assembled company, said Juliet, to "speculate whether it was the preacher's whiskers, which had a funny way of wagging up and down when he ate, or our uncle's peculiar method of 'making an eye' at us to enduce discipline that had started us going [laughing]."[39]

In spite of her wish for her daughters to associate only with society's better elements, and her own efforts never to sink to the level of common folks, Susan Humphries never kowtowed to the rich and mighty. Instead, Juliet observed, her mother preserved for herself a "quiet aloofness that won for her sometimes the name of being cold, critical, difficult to understand." She was difficult to understand, her daughter continued, because she knew things so well that she took it for granted that other people shared her competence in all matters. There existed no danger of a child misunderstanding her, said Juliet, because her mother knew that "children did not know things, and she was never too busy, nor too ill—and she was very often ill—to stop and explain. And when she explained once you knew." After she had grown up, Juliet often wished she had asked her mother about more matters and "taken more to heart" the things she had told her.[40] Juliet did note that the Humphries sisters never lost their "early implanted taste for refining influences" given to them by their mother. The gentle guidance of their mother gave the daughters "an advantage so immense as to be practically incalculable," she added.[41]

Despite Susan Humphries earnest efforts to ensure her children were cultured, her daughters' position in society remained precarious at best. Juliet noted that she and her sisters were not genteel, but were attractive, talented, and poor. This made them a "fine target for village gossips and for the slings and arrows of outrageous fortune as dealt out by more fortunate girls who have fathers and big brothers and money and 'social postion,'" she added.[42] Juliet remembered that the first time she realized her family was not "in the push" with society came when she attended the Rockville school system, which, by the 1860s, had established a graded school system with primary, intermediate, grammar, and high school levels.[43] "Education [in Rockville]," said Juliet, "was not despised as it was in many pioneer communities, many of the women whom I knew in early childhood, including my own mother, had been to 'boarding school,' and many of the men were college men."[44] Although she called herself a "very dilatory pupil," Strauss had an advantage over other students, as she had been taught to read and write at home by her mother. "I think I never studied a lesson in my life," Juliet admitted, "but I had something more valuable than schooling by way of education—the close companionship of a cultured mother who had a vocation for teaching and who devoted her whole life to the care and education of her children."[45]

She had no trouble in the departments covered by her mother at home, which even included a bit of Latin grammar, but Juliet despaired at solving mathematical questions and faced being left back a grade if she was unable to solve some math problems assigned her by her teacher. Stumped by subtraction, multiplication, and long division, she went for help to the usual source: her mother. At first Susan Humphries attempted to explain the mystery of math to her daugher, but failed. "When my mother found out that I couldn't work the problems and would be 'turned back' if I did not produce them, worked out on my slate," said Juliet, "she did what all mothers do in such desperate cases—worked them herself. I appeared at school the next morning with my slate closely covered with neat, accurate figures."

Her sudden wizardy at math made Juliet a popular figure, especially with boys eager to copy her answers to what were considered by them as rather difficult problems. Suddenly, one the boys paused in copying the answers long enough to ask Juliet how she knew the answers on her slate were correct? The following conversation ensued:

> "My mother helped me," I said. The ugly boy raised a great jeer—"oh, come on, fellers," he said, "I bet they ain't right—we'd jest as well copy hen-scratching'—yer mother!—why my paw can't even work 'em!" I was so dashed by his ridicule and my own sudden loss of newly-acquired prestige that I had no heart to defend my mother's mathematical work, and even later, when the problems turned out to be right to the letter, I did not feel relieved, and my heart lay like lead in my bosom when the boys yelled as I climbed the stile, feeling horribly awkward and conspicuous: "Oh, her mother gits her examples; who ever heard of the like?"[46]

The boys may have doubted her competence at math, but realized over the years that Juliet possessed a flair for English, particularly when it came to compositions. Her skill at writing became so well known with her schoolmates that "lazy boys" who waited until the last minute to complete their assignments sought her out to "put ginger" in their essays by contributing a paragraph or two. Miss Julia Hughes, Juliet's high school teacher, knew her pupil's writing style and soon discovered the ruse. She attempted to put a stop to the practice by returning papers to students with a blue pencil striking out entire paragraphs with the word "Gyp" in parenthesis beside them. "Finally," Juliet noted, "one boy got his composition back marked 'all Gyp'—and this settled matters for a while at least."[47]

Her flair for composition also caught the attention of a Rockville native who would do much to influence Juliet's subsequent career as a columnist: John Hanson Beadle. Beadle, who had come to Rockville with his family as a young boy and had attracted widespread attention from the community for his ability to recite the entire New Testament, had purchased the *Rockville Tribune* in April 1879 from Joseph B. Cheadle, a lawyer and later a member of Congress. Before assuming control of the Parke County weekly newspaper, which competed for subscribers in the community of approximately two thousand residents against the *Rockville Republican*, Beadle had served for a time as a private in the Union army, worked as an editorial writer for the *Evansville Journal*, served as Western correspondent for the *Cincinnati Commercial*, produced articles for a number of magazines and newspapers in New York City, and authored a book on his travels in the West titled *Western Wilds*. Strouse, who first worked for Beadle to learn the printing trade, regarded his boss as "the most remarkable man" he had ever known, noting that this editor of a little weekly in a small country town "could recite the *Iliad* in either Greek or English, and take up the sonorous lines of the 'Odes of Horace' at any place and quote them." Formerly a newspaper that supported the Republican party, the *Rockville Tribune* under Beadle pursued a more independent course refusing, for example, to support a third term for President Ulysses S. Grant and balking at the GOP call for an increase in the tariff.[48]

In December 1879 Beadle attended a literary exercise at the high school. In his report on the exercise for the *Tribune*, he had high praise for an essay titled "Chains" read by Juliet as editor of the school's newspaper. The work, Beadle wrote, contained "many sterling truths" expressed in "an easy, graceful style which is all her own."[49] Juliet vividly remembered Beadle's presence at the school event. Early into her reading she felt "that brilliant one eye of his fairly boring a hole through me." And while the newspaper editor found Juliet's work very appealing, older people in the audience were shocked by its frank nature. "The preachers always fidgeted around," Juliet recalled, "and the nice ladies in their rustling black silk frocks coughed apologetically behind their folded handkerchiefs—but Miss Hughes, our teacher, lived before her time and so she just turned me loose to say what I pleased."[50]

After the literary exercise was over, Beadle called upon Juliet's mother, Susan Humphries, and asked her if she realized her daugher possessed such a talent for literature. Beadle had seen in the young girl's work, her future husband Isaac Strouse said, much more than the "juvenile pedantry and very ordinary stock phrases which the 'editor' herself always insisted were most prominent in it." Beadle told Humphries that her daughter "should have the opportunity of seeing her work in print."[51] At first, Juliet's mother was "rather shocked" at the idea of having one of her daughters doing anything of a public nature, instead wishing only that they possess "good horse sense and be able to do something for a living." Susan Humphries, however, was "progressive for the times" according to Juliet, and agreed to let her middle daugher contribute to the *Rockville Tribune* and also learn shorthand as a possible trade.[52]

On 18 March 1880 *Rockville Tribune* readers were treated to an entertaining report on a roller skating party that included members of the community's elite society, which became a favorite target for Juliet's pen through the years, perhaps her way of repaying those who had snubbed her family in the past. The article, which appeared on the newspaper's front page, was signed "La Gitana," the nom de plume suggested for Juliet by Beadle. The first-person report notes that the author had chanced to be on the town's north side when to the writer's "astonishment" there arose a mighty rumbling. The article continues:

Urged by curiosity up the stairs I groped through a narrow hall and soon gazed with startled vision on the glories of the "skating rink." And *such* a vision! Rockville fashionables raised two inches above their usual elevation! The aristocracy on skates! Said I to myself, "were they not fast enough before?" I saw noble manhood converted into floating grace. I saw rude jostling pass for easy elegance. I saw boisterous falls, ugly falls, headlong lunges, awkward strokes, collisions, bumped heads, etc., made a subject of amusement for our older ladies. I saw a dignified business man scramble and beat the air and finally come down at a lady's feet in an elegant manner. I saw a handsome young lady, skating with her arms folded, suddenly become possessed of a mind to be seated, and she had no difficulty in finding a seat![53]

Concluding her first of many pieces for the *Rockville Tribune*, Juliet turned from observing the pratfalls of those involved to the hypocrisy she saw in their actions. She noted that she had been to many dances and heard preachers warn of dancing as "wicked, very, very wicked." But of course, there was not harm in roller skating, she said. "Look about and see the respectability of the skating rink," she wrote. "I could not but say softly to myself, "here's the church, here's the steeple, here's the *priest* and here's *all his people*! But there's no harm in skating on rollers—a blessing on rollers!"[54]

In addition to Beadle's assistance with her pseudonym, Juliet had help in keeping her writing identity secret from the community from another source, Isaac Strouse, who had been working at the *Tribune* for three years learning the printer's trade under the editor's tutelage in an attempt to "escape the daily drag of school which had become intolerable." Beadle had given Juliet's story on the skating rink to Strouse and suggested that he transfer it into type himself when no one else was in the office to guard against any disclosure of the author's identity. "The bond of secrecy thus established between the writer of that dainty and practically perfect manuscript was perhaps," said Strouse, "the most impelling of the mutual attractions which we found in each other."[55] It was an attraction, however, that had an unusual start. The two of them had lived in the same town and attended the same school, but it took a party to bring the duo together.

Notes

[1] John H. Beadle, "History of Parke County," in H. W. Beckwith, *History of Vigo and Parke Counties, Together with Historic Notes on the Wabash Valley* (Chicago: H. H. Hill and N. Iddings, Publishers, 1880), 29.

[2] Ibid., 29–30. See also, Isaac Strouse, *Parke County Indiana Centennial Memorial* (Rockville, Ind.: Rockville Chautauqua Association, 1916), 9; Maurice Murphy, "Some Features of the History of Parke County," *Indiana Magazine of History* 12 (June 1916): 150–51; Richard Simons, "Christening a Rock," *Indianapolis Star Magazine*, 5 April 1953; and "Glorious Days of Rockville In History Recalled in Observance of Centennial," *Indianapolis News*, 20 February 1924.

[3] Beadle, "History of Parke County," 30.

[4] Strouse, *Parke County Indiana Centennial Memorial*, 76.

[5] Emma Lou Thornbrough, *Indiana in the Civil War, 1850–1880* (1965; reprint, Indianapolis: Indiana Historical Society, 1989), 1.

[6] Murphy, "Some Features of the History of Parke County," 146.

[7] "Squibs and Sayings," *Rockville Tribune*, 22 January 1918.

[8] The Country Contributor, "Ideas of a Plain Country Woman," *Ladies' Home Journal*, April 1908.

[9] Murphy, "Some Features of the History of Parke County," 108.

[10] Juliet V. Strauss, "The Chronicles of a Queer Girl," *Ladies' Home Journal*, August 1907.

[11] Strauss, *The Ideas of a Plain Country Woman*, 186.

[12] "Hoosier Conservationist: Juliet V. Strauss," *Outdoor Indiana* (May 1944): 9.

[13] Robert H. Wiebe, *The Search for Order, 1877–1920* (New York: Hill and Wang, 1967), 2–3. Wiebe notes that those living in these small communities may have depended upon a larger city for markets and supplies, but they still were able to "retain the sense of living largely to themselves," living lives by the rhythms imposed by a farm life. Ibid.

[14] Strauss, *The Ideas of a Plain Country Woman*, 31.

[15] The Country Contributor, "The Ideas of a Plain Country Woman,"

Ladies' Home Journal, July 1908. The Rockville Town Board finally prohibited hogs from roaming free on city streets in 1870. The system, whereby people were given ten cents for every stray hog or cow brought to a "stray pen," proved a great temptation for Rockville boys of that time. There were instances of boys turning their own hogs and cows loose for some other boy to take to the stray pen and then the two youngsters would divide the money collected for finding the animals. See Strouse, *Parke County Centennial Memorial*, 83.

[16] Madison, *The Indiana Way*, 197.

[17] Mayo Fesler, "Secret Political Societies in the North during the Civil War," *Indiana Magazine of History* 14 (September 1918):183–84. For overviews on the tense atmosphere in the nineteenth state during the Civil War, see also, Thornbrough, *Indiana in the Civil War Era*, and Gilbert R. Tredway, *Democratic Opposition to the Lincoln Administration in Indiana* (Indianapolis: Indiana Historical Bureau, 1973).

[18] Murphy, "Some Features of the History of Parke County," 149.

[19] The Country Contributor, "The Ideas of a Plain Country Woman," *Ladies' Home Journal*, June 1910.

[20] "Squibs and Sayings," *Rockville Tribune*, 22 January 1918.

[21] See, The Country Contributor, "Ideas of a Plain Country Woman," *Ladies' Home Journal*, December 1906, and Murphy, "Some Features of the History of Parke County," 156. Murphy described McNutt as a Presbyterian minister of "talent and most lovable character." Ibid.

[22] The Country Contributor, "Ideas of a Plain Country Woman," *Ladies' Home Journal*, April 1910.

[23] Strauss, *The Ideas of a Plain Country Woman*, 226.

[24] Isaac Strouse, "In Memoriam," *Rockville Tribune*, 14 January 1903.

[25] Strauss, *The Ideas of a Plain Country Woman*, 32.

[26] Strauss, "The Chronicles of a Queer Girl," *Ladies' Home Journal*, November 1907.

[27] "Squibs and Sayings," *Rockville Tribune*, 22 January 1918.

[28] The Country Contributor, "The Ideas of a Plain Country Woman," *Ladies' Home Journal*, December 1906.

[29] The Country Contributor, "The Ideas of a Plain Country Woman," *Ladies' Home Journal*, June 1913.

[30] Strauss, *The Ideas of a Plain Country Woman*, 32.

[31] The Country Contributor, "The Ideas of a Plain Country Woman,"

Ladies' Home Journal, January 1907.

[32] Strauss, *The Ideas of a Plain Country Woman*, 174–75.

[33] The Country Contributor, "The Ideas of a Plain Country Woman," *Ladies' Home Journal*, June 1913.

[34] The Country Contributor, "The Short and Simple Annals of the Poor," *Indianapolis News*, 21 November 1903.

[35] Strauss, "The Chronicles of a Queer Girl," *Ladies' Home Journal*, July 1907.

[36] Strauss, *The Ideas of a Plain Country Woman*. 198–99.

[37] See, Strauss, "The Chronicles of a Queer Girl," *Ladies' Home Journal*, July 1907, and Marcia F. S. Ott, "Some Memories of My Mother," in *Rockville Tribune Memorial Supplement*, 4 June 1918.

[38] The Country Contributor, "The Ideas of a Plain Country Woman," *Ladies' Home Journal*, October 1907.

[39] Strauss, *The Ideas of a Plain Country Woman*, 33.

[40] Strauss, "The Chronicles of a Queer Girl," *Ladies' Home Journal*, November 1907.

[41] Strauss, "The Chronicles of a Queer Girl," *Ladies' Home Journal*, July 1907.

[42] The Country Contributor, "Ideas of a Plain Country Woman," *Ladies' Home Journal*, October 1907.

[43] Strouse, *Parke County Indiana Centennial Memorial*, 16. Strouse noted that he knew from "painful personal experience" that whipping students in Rockville schools following the Civil War was as much a part of "the teacher's work as any other thing in the daily routine." Whippings were administered to boys, and "big' girls, too," as a daily occurrence. Ibid. See also, Beadle, "History of Parke County." 52.

[44] "Squibs and Sayings," *Rockville Tribune*, 22 January 1918.

[45] Isaac Strouse, "Reminiscences About Life of Country Contributor," *Indianapolis News*, 5 June 1926.

[46] Strauss, "The Chronicles of a Queer Girl," *Ladies' Home Journal*, November 1907.

[47] Strouse, "Reminiscences About Life of Country Contributor," *Indianapolis News*, 5 June 1926.

[48] See, John Miller, *Indiana Newspaper Bibliography* (Indianapolis: Indiana Historical Society, 1982), 353; Strouse, *Parke County Indiana Cen-*

tennial Memorial, 40, 56; Strouse, "Reminiscences About Life of Country Contributor," *Indianapolis News*, 10 April 1926; and Beckwith, *History of Vigo and Parke Counties*, 127-30.

[49] "Half Yearly Exercises," *Rockville Tribune*, 25 December 1879.

[50] Strouse, "Reminiscences About Life of Country Contributor," *Indianapolis News*, 5 June 1926.

[51] Strouse, "Reminiscences About Life of Country Contributor," *Indianapolis News*, 10 April 1926.

[52] Strouse, "Reminiscences About Life of Country Contributor," *Indianapolis News*, 5 June 1926.

[53] "At the Rink," *Rockville Tribune*, 18 March 1880.

[54] Ibid.

[55] Strouse, "Reminiscences About Life of Country Contributor," *Indianapolis News*, 10 April 1926.

Chapter Two
THE MARRIAGE QUESTION

Early in the fall of 1879, a group of high school boys were sitting around a table at the offices of the *Rockville Tribune*. These boys naturally gravitated to the newspaper office, where, according to the paper's employee, Isaac Strouse, "pipes and tobacco were always at hand and could be smoked with immunity from parental displeasure." Born on 12 December 1859 in Rockville, Strouse had quit school at age sixteen to learn the printing trade in the offices of the *Indiana Patriot*, the forerunner of the *Rockville Tribune*. At first, Stouse and another boy had simply been charged with the task of printing editions of the newspaper on an old Washington hand press, and the Rockville native's ambition had only included becoming a typesetter and finding a job in Indianapolis. With Beadle's purchase of the *Rockville Tribune*, Strouse's horizons expanded. The veteran newspaperman agreed to take him on as a cub reporter, to review his work, and to give him informal lessons on the proper use of the English language. On this day in the newspaper office, Strouse, who had risen to become the newspaper's local editor, heard one of the boys proclaim Juliet Humphries as "the prettiest and smartest girl in Rockville." Although he had gone to school with Betty Humphries, the oldest of the Humphries' daughters, Strouse had never been introduced to the youngest member of the clan.[1]

A short time after the discussion in the newspaper office, Strouse finally met the then sixteen-year-old girl who was to become his wife at a party where he had the distinction of "being the oldest boy, as well as the only one not in school." Strouse spied his friend Betty Humphries sitting alone and went over to talk to her. After the two had been talking for awhile, another boy came over and demanded, in a friendly way, for Strouse to meet the other girls at the party and called over Betty's sister, Juliet. "Gyp [Juliet] came to our corner, bringing several of the other girls," said Strouse, "and we were all 'introduced,' though every one of us was born within a radius of a mile."[2] Strouse and Juliet fell into a long conversation, which included a discussion of books and poems they had recently read. Their shared love of literature, and the close bonds they formed through Juliet's "secret" work for the *Rockville Tribune*, helped begin a courtship that ended in marriage.

By the time Juliet did her first reporting job under her own name for the newspaper, she and the local editor were "regarded by themselves and everybody else as 'engaged,'" noted Strouse. And, in spite of the use of a pseudonym, the small community knew that it was Juliet Humphries who had written the skating rink article and several other pieces that had appeared in the newspaper. For her first assignment, Beadle sent Juliet to cover the Fine Arts Hall at the Parke County Fair. The fair was considered the one great event of the year and the *Rockville Tribune*, in order to scoop its rival newspaper, took its press out to the fairgrounds in order to issue a daily report on the fair's activities. According to Strouse, his fiancée had a bit of trouble at first with her assignment. Beadle, needing her copy, sent Strouse to secure her report. The local editor found her with a pencil posed to her lips and a blank notebook in her lap as she sat gazing at the quilts, breads, pies, canned fruits, and other articles that jammed the Fine Arts Hall. Sensing her quandary, Strouse advised Juliet to make general comments on the exhibits and not to give particulars. "O, that's easy," she responded. The couple walked over to the *Rockville Tribune*'s tent and she wrote such a fine article that Beadle told her "it was much better than anything he could have done, although he was a newspaper man of many years experience," noted Strouse.[3]

Unfortunately for Juliet, her work on the Parke County newspaper brought with it little financial remuneration. "I wanted the money to buy my wedding frock and a few other things," she said.

"There was no help for it."[4] At the age of seventeen, Juliet left school without receiving her high school degree and successfully passed the examination to become a teacher. In those days in Indiana, the state had no mandatory standards for teachers, with teaching licenses (like that given to Juliet) granted by county superintendents to those candidates who successfully passed written tests.[5] In addition to the written test, in order to gain a teaching job in Parke County Juliet had to obtain the signatures of a majority of the patrons in the school district. She had varying degrees of success with her neighbors: one man railed at her that her proper place was in the kitchen, not teaching school, and another offered to marry her as an alternative to signing her paper. Her father's legacy helped with one man, known in the area for his tendency to get drunk on election day and pick fights with fellow voters. The man, however, remembered that Juliet's father had been "a mighty good Democrat!" and agreed to help her by signing her paper and obtaining signatures from his other neighbors.[6]

Her stint as an educator lasted only a short time. "Under different circumstances I think I might have succeeded fairly well as a teacher," Juliet said, "for I did know what was in the books and I had a faculty for general information, which is what is often sadly lacking in a teacher. I could interest the children." She received help in disciplining any wayward boys from the oldest boy in the class, Henry, whom she befriended. "Soon he 'licked' every boy in school for me and we had fair order," Juliet said.[7] Instead of continuing her teaching career, however, she quit her job when she married Strouse. The nuptials, which took place on 22 December 1881, did not proceed without some disapproval—from the bride's family at least. Traveling to her job as a teacher one day in her uncle's wagon, she informed him that she intended to marry a man whose life's work was to be a newspaper editor. The uncle solemnly chewed on a piece of straw for a moment before telling his niece: "Jule, don't you know that being an editor is the orneriest business in the world?"[8]

Strouse, who at the time of his marriage to Juliet had gone over to the rival *Rockville Republican* to take a job as a printer at a higher salary, discovered that his new wife possessed not only writing talent, but an independent mind as well. On their wedding day the couple had received as presents such items as a set of silver spoons, a porcelain tea set, table linen, a lamb's wool comforter, and twenty-five gold dollars from the groom's father. Also, the uncle who had wondered about the wisdom of marrying a newspaper editor had "accepted the inevitable" and had given the couple as a wedding present an elaborate illustrated family Bible, which included an illuminated marriage certificate at the beginning of the family record. In the record, Juliet inscribed: "Isaac Rice Strauss was born December 12, 1863." Many years before, Strouse's father had "Americanized" his family's name from the German Strauss to Strouse. Throughout the rest of her life, Juliet used for her married name the old German spelling (Strauss), while her husband kept the newer version (Strouse). "She never would write our name as it was written by my father after he changed the spelling to compel the people of a typical Hoosier pioneer community to call him 'Strouse,'" noted her husband.[9]

The newlyweds endured a rough beginning to their years together. In the summer of 1882 they were both stricken with typhoid fever when an epidemic hit Rockville. With Strouse unable to go to work, and hence earn an income, the couple moved in with Strauss's mother, a woman for whom her son-in-law had a world of respect. "I have not spoken of this unequaled woman as my 'mother-in-law' a half dozen times in all my life," he observed. "I never could apply a name, so long the object of jokes and jibes, to such a woman." With Susan Humphries' able care, the young couple survived their bout with illness, but it took until autumn for Strouse to feel well enough to be up and about (his wife, whose sickness was far worse than his, was still confined to her sickbed but convalescent). Riding to the fairgrounds with his father, Strouse came across his former employer, Beadle. Taking Strouse aside, Beadle informed him that the "exigencies of journalism have made it imperative that I have a partner." The editor had fallen on hard times in his competition with Rockville's other two newspapers, the *Rockville Republican*, which (not surprisingly) supported the Republican party, and the *Parke County Signal,* which allied itself with the Democrats. Beadle's lack of business skills and some unfortunate hiring decisions that curtailed his ability to take freelance writing projects prompted him to ask his former employee to take a half-interest in the paper for $800. "Had he said $800,000," said Strouse, "the price to me would have amounted to the same kind of a proposal." Aware of the newlyweds' financial difficulties, Beadle arranged for Strouse's brother David to contribute $300, which he required to make the *Rockville Tribune* solvent again, and agreed to take a personal note from Strouse for the remaining $500. Strouse was more than happy to accept the offer and rode home to share the "glorious news" with his family. "How it heartened all of us!" he said. Not only did it mean some hopes of financial security for the young couple, but Beadle's kind offer (Strouse later learned that no mortgage had been made against his interest in the newspaper) would also provide Strauss the opportunity once again to utilize her writing talents.[10]

Beadle and Strouse announced their new partnership to the community in the pages of the *Rockville Tribune* on 10 November 1882. "It shall be our earnest endeavor to make it a live paper," the coeditors said, "containing all the local and a fair share of the general news, and for the next year we expect to make a specialty of home interests, in the schools, churches and business of the town and county."[11] Country weekly newspapers like the *Rockville Tribune* dominated journalism in the Hoosier state and the nation during the late nineteenth century. From 1870 to 1890, the number of community weeklies serving towns of less than ten thousand people in the county tripled in size from four thousand to twelve thousand. The phenomenal growth could be attributed to the modest capital investment it took to start a weekly newspaper in a small town.[12] Most towns could even boast of having two newspapers to choose from—one supporting the Democratic party and the other endorsing the Republican party. This happy circumstance came about as a result of the strong partisan nature of Indiana politics at this time and a legal advertis-

ing law requiring government notices to be published in two newspapers that represented political parties receiving the highest vote
totals in the last general election.[13] Politics was important to Strouse
(he gradually moved the *Rockville Tribune* from a nominally independent stance to one that solidly backed the Democratic party), but he
had to concentrate on other matters first to get the newspaper back
on its feet. Just the simple act of putting out a newspaper often meant
heavy labor with a small staff, slowly churning out pages by brute
force, typically with a Washington hand press. County editors in those
days, one practitioner of the art observed, served as "editor, reporter,
proof reader, solicitor, collector and general roustabout."[14]

One of the first steps Strouse took to improve the *Rockville
Tribune's* position in the community was to move its offices from its
location on the south side, a place "shunned by the up-and-coming
progressives and sought by the slothful, or down-and-outers in the
town's business affairs," to an upstairs location on the town square.
To brighten the newspaper's look, Strouse removed a number of "dead
ads," reduced its size from eight columns to five columns, and expanded the weekly from four to twelve pages, which included a literary supplement. He also crowded into the newspaper "'local' and 'feature' articles written by Mrs. Strauss [his wife] and her knowing, sensible mother—all of it making a wonderful change in the old sheet,"
Strouse noted, adding that "before long we began to issue extra pages
and a special Christmas number."[15] As he took on more and more
responsibilities at the newspaper (Strouse became the *Rockville
Tribune's* sole owner and editor in 1889), the newspaperman also
found himself calling upon his wife time and time again to provide
more copy to enliven the newspaper's columns, including a department of "Local Fables" written in the style of Aesop.

One of the first fables Strauss produced for the newspaper involved the printer's towel, a ubiquitous part of every printing shop.
One day when she had stopped by the newspaper office to help put
out the paper, Strauss asked the young printer's devil working there
for a towel to wash her hands. The youth found the towel and "shoved

it toward her very much as he would a board," Strouse noted. Strauss, who decided to use some white print paper to wipe off her hands instead of the filthy towel, was inspired to write the following fable for the *Rockville Tribune:*

> *Local Fables—No. 2*
> A printer thus complained to his towel:
> "Why art thou so devilish stiff as to whack off my fingers when I wipe them on thee?" The patient towel made no answer. Several days afterwards the printer's wife happened in and, seeing it, hired a dray and had the towel taken to an adjacent millpond and washed. The next day when the printer approached it, the towel cried out: "Avaunt thou ungrateful cuss: When the filth from thy hands hath rendered me vile, thou scornest me; no I am no friend of thine."
> *Moral*
> Men often scorn what they themselves have polluted.[16]

Typically for her, Strauss later tried to downplay her early contributions to the newspaper's revitalization. "The editor would come home tired and careworn from his struggles with the old Washington hand press," she said, "and his interviews with patronizing subscribers who wanted to pay in pithy turnips or green stovewood cut two inches too long for our little 'early breakfast' wood cook stove—and I hadn't the heart to refuse when he asked me if I couldn't write something to brighten up the paper."[17]

Just a few weeks before the birth of their first child, Marcia, born on 20 June 1883, Strauss earned her first money for her writing. With Beadle out of town on a freelance writing assignment, Strouse, in charge of the newspaper, was stopped on his way out of the office by a man who had recently returned to town to attend a relative's funeral. The man handed the editor a ten dollar bill and said that he wanted an obituary of his relative in that week's *Rockville Tribune.* Strouse told the man there was usually no charge for such notices, but added that it might be impossible to get the sketch into the newspaper because, in order to get the edition out on time, Strouse had to work the press himself. The man persisted, however, and Strouse took the money, had it converted into a five-dollar gold piece, and ran home. Once there he promised his wife that she could have the money if she wrote the sketch in time for that week's newspaper. She got the money.[18]

Strauss proved herself to be a tower of support for everyone involved in the operation of the country newspaper. Edmund Beadle, a nephew of John Beadle who started at the *Rockville Tribune* as an apprentice printer and eventually rose to become its owner in 1919, remembered that during the Rockville and Bridgeton fairs the *Rockville Tribune* printed between two thousand and three thousand premium lists. "No sooner would the ink be dry than the sheets were carried to Mrs. Strauss for folding and binding at home," said Beadle. "She with needle and thread gave every spare moment she could from household work and care of her small daughters [her second daughter, Sarah Katherine, was born on 3 January 1887] to the tedious task of folding and binding the premium lists."[19]

Strauss also provided leadership for the newspaper at a time in journalism when females were a rare sight in newsrooms. The dirty and often noisy newspaper offices were considered "off limits" for genteel ladies.[20] For Strauss, however, there was no alternative; she often had to take over management of the *Rockville Tribune* for a week or two at a time while her husband, an avid outdoorsman, took hunting trips into the countryside. "There were so many interesting habitués about the shop in those days of hand work and easy living—it seemed as if there was more time to be lazy, talented and happy," she said. Although she had to often deal with such problems as drunk printers, Strauss could turn for help to such persons as Doug Smith, Frank Howard, Will Mason, and others for copy to fill the paper. As for printers, she noted that "one could always pick up somebody and put him on his mettle to save the day if somebody fell by the wayside."[21]

Although poor and struggling to repay the $300 debt owed his brother David, Strouse noted that the one outstanding recollection of those early days of his married life was "one of constant fun and frolic."[22] There may have been little or no cash on hand from subscribers, but when it came to farm products taken in kind for a subscription to the newspaper, "we were opulent beyond the wealthiest of our townspeople." The Strouse household also received an abundant supply of reading material. Such periodicals as the *North American Review*, *Atlantic*, *Scribner's*, the *Magazine of American History*, and the *Independent Youth's Companion* were obtained in exchange for advertising or reviews. With free passes provided by railroad lines, the young couple could also travel to Terre Haute for performances at the opera house.[23] Angry or resentful comments against the couple, said Strouse, were given a "humorous turn" in their work for the newspaper. When a woman made some snide comments about a new blue dress Strauss had received from her husband, she used the incident as inspiration for the following poem:

> And so you made fun of my 'duds,' little friend,
> And called me a dowdy, a guy and a fright,
> And remarked, if I'm not very much misinformed
> That I never had anything on that was right.
>
> Perhaps you were right, for my pocketbook's slim,
> And dresses with me don't grow upon trees,
> More's the pity, for then you could pick me one, see,
> A pretty gown blossom that could not but please.
>
> A very sweet lady with very good taste,
> And a very good heart too, at least we suppose
> That very good ladies with very good hearts
> Make fun of their poor little neighbor's 'good cloze.'
>
> 'Twas a much great poet than I, little friend,
> Who wished for some power the giftie to gie us
> To see ourselves in our own looking glasses
> Exactly as such little friends as you see us.

But that wish was not granted, my dear little friend,
Or we'd know when our bustle is all out of whack,
Or could tell with precision whenever our gown
Is 'sagging' a mile and a half in the back.

What a happy little woman was old Mother Eve;
Even after her exit from Eden's fair gate;
There wasn't a soul upon earth who could giggle,
And say that her fig leaf wasn't on very straight.

If I cross before your death's dark stream, little friend,
Leaving only my body, all senseless and white.
Come and help make my shroud, that for once folks may see
me
Gotten up quite regardless and looking all right.[24]

Strouse may have seen his early years of married life as an un-paralleled joy, but the struggles of raising a family on a meager income sometimes took their toll on Strauss, who admitted that she spent her early married years "in intense bitterness over poverty."[25] Even though she did all she could to help at the newspaper office, most of Strauss's time was spent in the kitchen, "and there was not much outlook from its one window," she noted. Strouse often worked to eleven in the evening at the *Rockville Tribune*; he had to, he admitted, because he never could "resist the temptation to take my shotgun and go when Frank Howard, a brilliant, byronic lawyer . . . would propose a quail hunt."[26] Left to care for her two children and deal with the daily grind of housework, Strauss's hardships were many: she never owned anything "pretty" to wear, the house was meagerly furnished, and she had to make for her children "such garments as I could devise from the outworn raiments of their elders and such bargains as I could pick up at the village store."[27] These difficulties never seemed to register with her husband. "At least," said Strauss, "it never occurred to him to compare anything we had with what our friends had. He never knew that I was the shabbiest, the most overworked of all our family and friends. It never stung him that we couldn't dress our children as well as other people, or send them away to school, or travel with them, or give them glimpses of the world."[28]

The pressures of making ends meet came to a head one Christmas, a holiday she said she ruined for her family by giving way to a "rush of discouragement and envy." Strauss had worked hard to ensure that her two daughters had sufficient presents for the holiday. When her husband came home on Christmas Eve, he casually tossed a package into his wife's lap and said: "There's your present." Strauss did not open the package because she knew "instinctingly that it was something cheap and ugly." As her husband settled in for the evening, he began to talk about a diamond necklace that one of the couple's friends, rich in the lumber trade, had bought for his wife. "A hot wave of fury seemed to pass over my soul," Strauss said. "I sat trying not to say anything, not to cry, not to shriek out as I felt like doing." Instead of saying anything to her husband, Strauss opened her present and discovered that it contained a piece of navy-blue calico—enough material to make a kitchen dress.

This proved to be too much for Strauss, who angrily asked her husband: "So you bought your poor drudge of a wife a kitchen dress?" As Strouse looked at his wife in amazement, she burst into a fit of weeping that lasted the remainder of the night. The couple did not speak to each other all Christmas day. Strauss took it on herself to put matters right and forgive her husband's foibles. "It was 'up to me' to be clever for both of us, to see the humorous side of it, to know him for the honest blunderer that he was, and 'make allowance,'" she said.[29] Later, she ruefully wondered why it was that a woman falls in love with a man "just because he is masculine . . . then puts in a lifetime of trying to make a house cat of him, jamming him into a dress suit by force and hauling him off to social 'functions?'" For the same reason, she supposed, that a man marries a "pretty, dainty, frivolous, society girl and expects her to 'settle down.'"[30]

In spite of the financial difficulties that plagued the family, Strauss's daughters had happy memories of their childhood. Marcia, the oldest, who followed in Strauss's footsteps by becoming a columnist for her hometown newspaper (the *Rockville Republican*), noted that her mother "bruised her heart and hands alike . . . to make the way smooth for her children. I early learned that any childish hurt we received hurt her inexpressibly worse." Like her mother before her, Strauss attempted to fill her daughters' lives with culture and learning. One of Marcia Strouse's earliest memories was of a summer's day when her mother took her and her sister to the home of a neighbor. Finding her friend gone, Strauss made herself at home, as was her custom, and sat down at her friend's old-fashioned piano and played and sang a sentimental ballad titled "Near the Lake Where Drooped the Willow." Their family had no piano, Marcia said, and the "ability to play on one was something tremendous in my eyes and something I had never suspected that she [Strauss] possessed."

In addition to music, Strauss introduced her daughters to quality literature, reading to them from the works of William Shakespeare and Charles Dickens. The family also enjoyed horseback rides (Strauss's favorite recreation), picnics, camping trips, moonlight carriage drives, and "gatherings of every kind" with relatives and friends. "We were all poor," said Marcia Strouse, "our own little family was perhaps the poorest of them, but how little they cared, those blessed unconventional people, how queer the old carriages looked, so they got to the picnic; how shabby the furniture was, so they were all together."[31] As Strauss herself related, she was surrounded during her married days by a "troupe of friends devoted to having a good time." Although spurned by the community's women's clubs and society functions, she was a "Royal Princess in this coterie. The witch brew of simple human play and pleasure wouldn't boil till I came and poured in sows' blood or other ingredients of primitive efficacy."[32]

With her husband's complete takeover as owner and editor of the *Rockville Tribune* in 1889, Strauss continued to provide assistance in whatever areas she could, contributing essays, poems, and other articles. The only piece of work she refused to tackle were editorials. Although politically in sympathy with her husband's support of the Democratic party, she personally disliked politics. No matter how "sick or unable to write I might be during all the years she constantly contributed to our paper she never would write a political editorial," said Strouse.[33] The only time Strouse could remember his wife deviating from this nonpartisan outlook came in 1896 when John Clark Ridpath, a well-known Hoosier educator, writer, and popular historian ran for Congress on the Democratic ticket. Ridpath, according to Strouse, had been "one of the first to recognize literary abilities in Juliet V. Strauss" and had always visited the couple when he came to Rockville. Because of her fondness for Ridpath, Strauss, according to her husband, worked tirelessly on her friend's behalf, attending rallies, decorating speaker's stands, and assisting other women in their auxiliary work. Strauss's efforts, which included helping feed hundreds of people who had attended a rally on Ridpath's behalf, were for naught; the Indiana historian lost to Republican George W. Faris by only 365 votes.

Strouse and his wife, through their longtime support of the Democratic party, also became good friends with United States senator John W. Kern and his wife and Indiana governor and vice president Thomas Marshall and his wife. Attending an Indiana Democratic Editorial Association meeting in Indianapolis in 1908, Strauss noted that the three couples were strolling over the grounds after dinner at one of the city's country clubs late in the evening when Mrs. Marshall discovered a four-leaf clover. A few steps later, Mrs. Kern and Strauss also found four-leaf clovers, the first either had ever found in their lives. The women gave the lucky charms to Marshall, then a candidate for Indiana governor, and Kern, vice-presidential candidate with perennial Democratic presidential contender William Jennings Bryan. Along with their possession of four-leaf clovers, the two candidates also happened to be standing in a position to see the new moon over their right shoulders. "The combination of fortuitous omens added to the high spirits of the ladies of the party," said Strauss, "at least, who confessed their respect for 'signs,' if not their belief in them, and as the men were feeling pretty good anyway, having listened all day to cheering reports from all parts of the state, this little coincidence of good luck chimed in happily with an optimistic mood." The charms worked for Marshall, who became the first Democratic governor in the Hoosier state since 1893 by defeating Republican James Watson, but the Bryan/Kern ticket went down in defeat to the GOP.[34]

Just a few years after her husband gained control of the newspaper, Strauss embarked on an ambitious new writing project. On 9 February 1893 Strauss wrote her first "Squibs and Sayings" column for the *Rockville Tribune*. At first, her husband had attempted to dissuade his wife from becoming responsible for a regular department. Although "delighted" with her idea, he warned her that in his experience such departments usually ran in country newspapers for only a few weeks or months at best. "I believe I can keep it up," Strauss said.[35] She was as good as her word; the front-page column ran in the newspaper every week until Strauss's death in 1918. And while Strauss eventually grew tired of the weekly grind involved in producing a column, her work for the *Rockville Tribune* led to something she always desired—a larger audience for her writing.

Notes

[1] Strouse, "Reminiscences About Life of Country Contributor," *Indianapolis News*, 10 May 1926. See also, "Isaac R. Strouse, Former Tribune Editor, Succumbs," *Rockville Tribune*, 5 December 1934.

[2] Strouse, "Reminiscences About Life of Country Contributor," *Indianapolis News*, 10 May 1926.

[3] "Reminiscence," *Rockville Tribune Memorial Supplement*, 4 June 1918.

[4] The Country Contributor, "The Ideas of a Plain Country Woman," *Ladies' Home Journal*, September 1909.

[5] Phillips, *Indiana in Transition*, 404. After 1899, responsibility for preparing examination questions for granting teaching licenses fell to the State Board of Education. Candidates could still choose to have their tests graded by county superintendents instead of the state with their license only valid within that area. This was the path followed by most elementary teachers until as late as 1920. Ibid., 404–5.

[6] Strouse, "Reminiscences About Life of Country Contributor," *Indianapolis News*, 17 April 1926.

[7] The Country Contributor, "The Ideas of a Plain Country Woman," *Ladies' Home Journal*, September 1909.

[8] Strouse, "Reminiscences About Life of Country Contributor," *Indianapolis News*, 24 April 1926.

[9] Ibid. See also, Strauss, *The Ideas of a Plain Country Woman*, 99–100.

[10] See Strouse, *Parke County Memorial*, 56, and Strouse, "Reminiscences About Life of Country Contributor," *Indianapolis News*, 24 April 1926.

[11] "To the Reading Public," *Rockville Tribune*, 10 November 1882. The announcement of the Beadle and Strouse partnership was marred by a typographical error in the masthead, where Strouse's name was misspelled as Srtouse. Ibid.

[12] Frank Luther Mott, *American Journalism, A History: 1690–1960* (New York: The MacMillan Company, 1962), 478. All one needed to start a country newspaper, Mott noted, was an old Washington hand press or a new hand-cranked cylinder press, a few cases of type, an imposing stone,

and for job work, a foot-powered press. Although founded with ease, these types of newspapers "were maintained with more difficulty," he added. Ibid.

[13] John E. Stempel and Richard D. Yoakam, "Communications Media," in Donald F. Carmony, editor, *Indiana: A Self-Appraisal* (Bloomington: Indiana University Press, 1966), 139–40, and Phillips, *Indiana in Transition*, 525–26. According to the Indiana Department of Statistics, the state in 1884 had 366 weekly newspapers as opposed to only 42 daily newspapers. By 1909, the total for weeklies had risen to 517 and the total for dailies stood at 172. Ibid., 526.

[14] H. S. K. Bartholomew, "Newspaper Work at the Turn of the Century," *Indiana Magazine of History* 35 (September 1939): 303–6.

[15] Strouse, "Reminiscences About Life of Country Contributor," *Indianapolis News*, 1 May 1926.

[16] Ibid. See also, "Local Fables—No. 2," *Rockville Tribune*, 18 January 1882.

[17] Strouse, "Reminiscences About Life of Country Contributor," *Indianapolis News*, 5 June 1926.

[18] "Reminiscence," *Rockville Tribune Memorial Supplement*, 4 June 1918.

[19] Edmund P. Beadle, "Mrs. Strauss and the Tribune," *Rockville Tribune Memorial Supplement*, 4 June 1918.

[20] Maurine H. Beasley and Shelia J. Gibbons, *Taking Their Place: A Documentary History of Women and Journalism* (Washington, D. C.: American University Press in cooperation with the Women's Institute for Freedom of the Press, 1993), 8. In helping her husband with the newspaper, Strauss was following a path tread by many women in America as far back as colonial times when women "assisted male relatives in printing and publishing shops that adjoined homes." Ibid.

[21] Strouse, "Reminiscences About Life of Country Contributor," *Indianapolis News*, 5 June 1926.

[22] Strouse, "Reminiscences About Life of Country Contributor," *Indianapolis News*, 8 May 1926.

[23] Strouse, "Reminiscences About Life of Country Contributor," *Indianapolis News*, 15 May 1926.

[24] Strouse, "Reminiscences About Life of Country Contributor," *Indianapolis News*, 8 May 1926. Those early struggling days of the *Rockville Tribune* placed their mark on Strauss. Reflecting on her work for the country newspaper before a meeting of the National Editorial Association in

Colorado Springs, Strauss, whose address was titled "A Woman's Experience in Journalism," warned readers of her column in the *Rockville Tribune* not to tell her that they admired her work if they had borrowed the newspaper. "The most contemptible form of stealing," she said, "is to steal entertainment you are too stingy to pay for. It is difficult to say which man is worse, the man who borrows or the man who loans. Don't hand your paper around—if the reading matter is good it is worth paying for." See Strouse, "Reminiscences About Life of Country Contributor," *Indianapolis News*, 5 June 1926.

[25] The Country Contributor, "The Ideas of a Plain Country Woman," *Ladies' Home Journal*, December 1909.

[26] Strouse, "Reminiscences About Life of Country Contributor," *Indianapolis News*, 1 May 1926.

[27] Strauss, *The Ideas of a Plain Country Woman*, 63.

[28] The Country Contributor, "The Ideas of a Plain Country Woman," *Ladies' Home Journal*, December 1909.

[29] Ibid.

[30] The Country Contributor, "Ideas of a Plain Country Woman," *Ladies' Home Journal*, August 1912.

[31] Marcia F. S. Ott, "Some Memories of My Mother," *Rockville Tribune Memorial Supplement*, 4 June 1918.

[32] The Country Contributor, "The Ideas of a Plain Country Woman," *Ladies' Home Journal*, September 1912.

[33] See, Strouse, "Reminiscences About Life of Country Contributor," *Indianapolis News*, 29 May 1926, and "Reminiscence," *Rockville Tribune Memorial Supplement*, 4 June 1918.

[34] Strouse, "Reminiscences About Life of Country Contributor," *Indianapolis News*, 29 May 1926.

[35] "Reminiscence," *Rockville Tribune Memorial Supplement*, 4 June 1918.

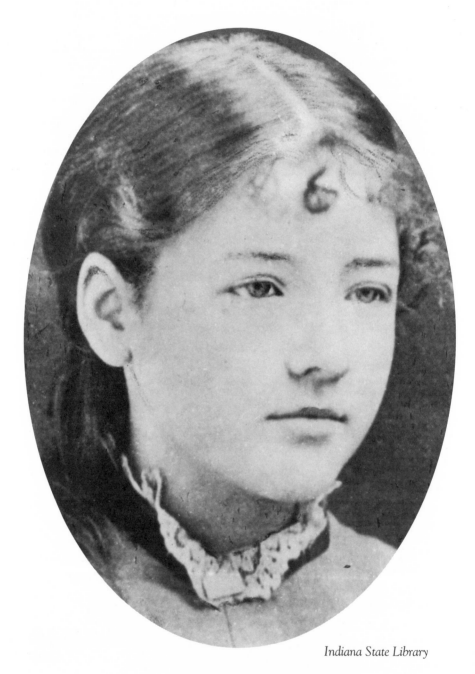

Juliet Virginia Humphries at age sixteen

Juliet Virginia Humphries and Isaac Strouse at the time of their marriage in 1880

Juliet Strauss and her first child, her daughter, Marcia, 1883.

The north side of downtown Rockville in the late nineteenth century

Juliet Strauss

George Cottman

William Herschell

Grouch Place, home of The Country Contributor
in Rockville, Indiana

Juliet Strauss during her days as
The Country Contributor

Frank McKinney "Kin" Hubbard,
creator of Abe Martin

John W. Kern

James Whitcomb Riley

Chapter Three
THE COPY BOOK

The *Rockville Tribune* for 9 February 1893 featured its usual blend of local news for the week and dispatches culled from a variety of other Hoosier newspapers. On its front page, the weekly reported that the bridge at Montezuma had recently been completed and an offer from the newspaper that it had for sale at its offices a complete set of the *Encyclopedia Britannica* for just $20 (the price included a year's subscription to the newspaper). Regular subscribers to the *Rockville Tribune* also were treated to a new feature, an unsigned column titled "Squibs and Sayings." That first of many columns to flow from Strauss's pen included her observation on why children of the day failed to learn how to read as well as they had in the past and the fashion question of whether or not to wear hoops under skirts. "Don't laugh: it sounds silly," noted Strauss, "but it is in reality this proposition: Common sense vs. fashion. Think of it, thinking women of today, and decide whether you will, for the sake of the caprice of a fashion, put back on the shackles of silliness that have bound your sex so long?"[1]

For the next twenty-five years, even when illness forced her to bed, Strauss produced her column for the newspaper. Her hard work on behalf of her husband's newspaper paid off. Even a competitor, the *Rockville Republican*, admitted that Strauss's weekly essays "have aided not a little in building up the reputation of the Tribune as one of the best country papers in Indiana."[2] Always seemingly busy at home taking care of her family, Strauss found that she could not "go out in society much—news was scarce and society items few and far between—so I had to 'dig out' what I wrote from my head."[3] In her column, she commented on all aspects of life in the Parke County community and beyond, everything including the appearance in Rockville of the first woman bicyclist, the annoying number of advertisements jammed into magazines, the tragedy that befalls a family when reduced to poverty, and the beauties of a spring day. The newspaper offered her the chance to explore her ideas on the worth of life as a homemaker as opposed to life in society. In one early column she argued that hard work only becomes drudgery when "one's physical strength is unequal to it, or when one's mind is allowed to dwell persistently upon its disagreeable features." Even the "homeliest tasks may be made wholesome," she said, "if the worker has plenty of strength, both of mind and body."[4]

Strauss also used incidents from her home life to enliven the column, a habit she followed in her subsequent work for other periodicals. She even got away with poking fun at the newspaper's owner, her husband, complaining one May that it was the time of year when a wife had to "exercise her Christian grace in listening to descriptions of the big bass that got away, heard in intervals of scaling the scant 'catch' of sunfish and goggle eyes, and warding off the stealthy advances of the cat . . . not to mention quieting sundry wails from the children, who insist upon 'watching,' and becoming chief mourners over every fish which is beheaded."[5]

The "Squibs and Sayings" column provoked responses, both positive and negative, from readers in the community. Strauss's remarks on a performance in Rockville by the Charles Hanford Company of Shakespeare's *Julius Caesar* provoked one outraged reader to write a letter of complaint, a piece Strauss termed as a "long, sarcastic, venomous criticism of me and my work," which was printed in the rival *Rockville Republican* newspaper.[6] In her "Squibs and Sayings" column, Strauss commented more on the audience than on the play. She noted that one amusing feature of the evening was the "anxiety with which some people watch certain others in order to take their cue. If certain people laugh, then the play is killing funny; if they applaud, then the acting is fine." What infuriated the *Rockville Republican* letter writer, however, was Strauss's flaying of the "unbound intellectual ambition" of a few women in the community. "There is nothing in the way of intellectual pursuit," Strauss wrote, "which a certain class of would-be intellectual women wont tackle. But alas, in thought as in dress, they are fearfully afraid they will be *de rigeuer.* So they pound their heads over books that they think they ought to read . . . and making sure of the opinions of others, whom they consider authority, before voicing their conclusions."[7]

Strauss's harsh words may have been prompted by the couple's exclusion from the community's literary scene. Rockville, like numerous other Hoosier cities during Indiana's golden age of literature stretching from 1880 to 1920, experienced a keen growth in literary clubs, which sprang into existence to minister to those afflicted with the writing bug.[8] "We had never been 'asked' to join either of the four literary clubs [in Rockville]," said Strouse, "a slight we could not help from feeling."[9] The lack of respect felt for Strauss's work, at least, is evident in the *Rockville Republican* letter to the editor, signed "Marc Antony" and featured on the newspaper's front page. "What I saw," the letter said of the people attending the play, "what each one saw, who is not infected with the venom of envy, was a bright, intelligent, well behaved audience. Neither did I notice any of that mental toadyism which was apparent to the writer of 'Squibs and Sayings.'" The letter went on to say it was both amusing and presumptuous that a person [Strauss] who was born and raised in Rockville, "who has been outside of the corporation only a few times, whose whole education was received in the common schools of this town, not even finishing the high school course, should set herself . . . up for the critic and censor not only of Rockville, but of the entire county." The letter concluded by advising the "Squibs and Sayings" columnist to form her own club of one to study the rules of grammar and rhetoric so "she would not so often offend good taste by such expressions as 'would-be intellectual women won't tackle,' &c., &c., &c."[10]

The harsh words against her printed in the *Rockville Republican* hurt Strauss, but she tried to put on a brave face before her friends. Shortly after the scathing letter against her had appeared in the newspaper, Strauss was walking uptown to purchase a dime's worth of beefsteak when she happened to run into Thomas Rice, a Rockville attorney and family friend. Rice held out his hand to his friend and said: "My dear girl, don't you let 'em down you—there are a whole lot of us who believe in you and who know that you are going to get there." Strauss smiled in response to her friend's encouragement and replied that she had been trying not to worry about the criticism leveled at her. "I feel something within me that keeps on whisperin'—greatness," she said. Actually, Strauss added, she had spoken falsely; she really "felt like 30 cents—but the quotation from [Charles] Dickens sprang to my lips and I said it." Although she took comfort from those people in town, like Rice, who expressed to her personally their delight in her writing, the harsh words directed at her continued to be a sore spot all of her life. "You would be surprised to know," Strauss later wrote, "how well a kind or helpful word . . . is remembered all a lifetime—and, too, how, though you may forgive them, the unkind word or act remains—a hurt that never quite heals."[11] Her branding by some in the community as a "dangerous individual" who might cause outsiders to think Rockville a queer place did, however, leave Strauss free to express her opinions without fear "because if nobody was going to notice them one might just as well experience the relief of getting rid of a lot of bottled up sentiment that seemed anxious to get out. So I just said them."[12]

A more public boost to Strauss's frayed feelings occurred at one of the literary clubs that ostracized her and her husband. Along with her comments on life in Parke County, her "Squibs and Sayings" column featured on occasion Strauss's poetry. She also found an outlet for her verse in the pages of the *Indianapolis Journal*, a publication dubbed as "one of the best journalistic friends Indiana writers ever had" by George S. Cottman, and a newspaper that helped launch the career of James Whitcomb Riley.[13] One day Strouse and his wife had been invited to attend a meeting of one of the town's literary clubs—only because the meeting happened to be held at the house of Strouse's brother—to hear an address by Colonel Thomas H. Nelson, a former Rockville attorney who had served as United States minister to Chile during the Lincoln administration. During his informal talk about American poetry before the club, Nelson took a moment to tell the audience: "You have here in your own little town a poet of whom you no doubt are proud, and who honors this occasion with her presence." He then recited from memory Strauss's poem "Indian Summer," which had been printed in the *Indianapolis Journal*:

> While walking slow with downcast eyes
> Under the Indian Summer skies,
>
> Following some sober reverie
> Lo! Some one came and walked with me!
>
> And as we walked in sunset's glow,
> A silent pair with footsteps slow,
>
> Fearing to trust our eyes to meet,
> A change came o'er the quiet street,
>
> And we were not ourselves; instead
> We were those lovers—long since dead—
>
> Who lived, or so the world still claims,
> Long years ago and bore our names.
>
> For was I not that little maid
> Who wore her hair in girlish braid,
>
> Not I, with tresses turning gray,
> Who walked with you this autumn day?
>
> And some one walked with me, I know,
> Whose dark eyes made me tremble so!
>
> A shadow with the face of him
> Whose memory makes my eyes grow dim.

Ah! Little dreamed the passerbys
Who doffed their hats as we drew nigh

That in the guise of human form
Two ghosts were walking arm-in-arm!

Two spirits as the sun sank low,
Back from the shores of long ago!

Around us fell through purple mist,
Leaves by the sun's last red rays kissed

From trees whose dusky boles were lifted
In air where golden dust was sifted.

We walked across enchanted ground,
None knew our footsteps made no sound.

The spell was brief, some words were spoken
And with those words the spell was broken;

Life stared into our dreaming faces,
Fast losing youth's entrancing graces,

And once more we were creatures human,
You were a man, and I a woman.

Love made us youth and maiden seem,
That love that was a dream—a dream!

How often in my sadder moods,
The sunlight on the autumn woods,

The moonlight on the sleeping town
Still stirs within my heart deep down

In memory's haunts regret and pain
And brings the dream of youth again.[14]

Along with having luck in getting her poems published, Strauss tried her hand at short stories and sold a few to such publications as the *Indianapolis Journal*, *Indianapolis News*, and *Demorest's Magazine*. Feeling unsure about her writing, Strauss turned for help to a person who had become a successful central Indiana freelance writer—George S. Cottman. Born in Indianapolis on 10 May 1857 Cottman had served as an apprentice printer at the *Indianapolis Sentinel*. Possessed with a love of history and a deftness with words, however, he soon turned his talents to making a living through writing. Traveling throughout the state on his faithful bicycle, he unearthed material on historical and natural subjects, which he turned into articles for the *Indiana Farmer*, *Indianapolis Journal*, *Indianapolis News*, and *Indianapolis Press*. Cottman, founder in 1905 of the quarterly *Indiana Magazine of History*, also became a key and active member of the Western Association of Writers, the authors' group that worked to promote "acquaintance and friendship among the literary fraternity." The organization, which was dominated throughout its approximately twenty-year existence by Hoosier writers, also worked to protect authors against so-called "piratical publishers."[15]

Strauss turned to Cottman in September 1896, asking for his opinion on some short stories she had written. "I take criticism very well," the budding author wrote the Indianapolis writer, "so if you have anything on your mind you would like to say to me I shall be glad to hear from you."[16] Strauss got her wish. In a return letter to the Rockville native, Cottman offered a lengthy critique of Strauss's work, telling her that he was taking such a detailed examination of her story "by reason of the new field which you give us a glimpse of, and also because of certain literary powers evinced in them which, if carefully directed, might, it seems to me, result in work of more than transient value." He also took the time to give his opinions on the state of Hoosier literature, writing:

> Indiana, both past and present . . . is very inadequately repre-
> sented in literature. Beyond our borders we are known, largely,
> through the works of [Edward] Eggleston and [James Whitcomb]
> Riley, and the general conception based on these writers, strength-
> ened by the widespread idea otherwise engendered, that Indiana
> always has been a commonwealth of mud-sills, is false. Conceding
> that Eggleston and Riley accurately portrayed certain types of char-
> acter indigenous to our soil, those types do not adequately stand
> for the state at large, either now nor at any past time. Our writers
> have, so far, failed to point out that there have been and are other
> equally interesting phases of life.
>
> Among intelligent readers how many are there who know of the
> world of . . . romance which existed all down the Ohio and Wa-
> bash valley in the days when those rivers were great arteries carry-
> ing tides of emigration into the heart of the new west. And how
> many know of the . . . picturesque character of those early popula-
> tions, made up, as they were, not only of pioneers of the ax and
> rifle, but 'jurists and statesmen, and ladies and gentlemen, of the
> old school' whom you so aptly speak of?[17]

The Indiana historian praised Strauss's ability to capture that
"picturesque character" of the state's early population he spoke of in
his letter. He had long thought that those phases of life, buried in
oblivion for so long, would at some time "prove a mine for some Indiana writer of fiction yet to come; and, so far as I am aware, you
[Strauss] are the first person on the ground with any indication of a
serious purpose." Cottman found, however, that Strauss needed to
work on two areas: her storytelling ability and developing her own
style. He offered the advice that art, or more specifically the story, is
"realism—the objective facts plus the imagination of the artist, who,
out of a sense of harmony, proportions, fitness, beauty, combines those
facts to serve his own purpose, and impressing into them meanings
of his own."[18]

Responding to Cottman's letter, Strauss agreed with his observation that she possessed a great fascination for portraying old times—a fascination so intense that she often, in writing, would "forget all about my plot and even have to scrape around to get a semblance of a story upon which to hang the incidents." She also shared with Cottman some of her frustration at trying to be both a housewife and writer and admitted that she had little spare time for outside reading. Perhaps thinking of the stinging rebukes she sometimes suffered from the hands of her fellow Rockville natives, she also expressed a strong aversion for the writing work she had become best known for: newspapers. She wrote Cottman: "I have read only in a desultory way. Written poetry because I couldn't help it. Done newspaper work for fifteen years because I had to (I *hate* it) and written in all eight stories five of which I have sold. If you knew me, you would see how useless it is to urge me to become methodical and have a motif. There isn't any you know."[19]

In the next year, Strauss continued to correspond with Cottman and shared with her fellow writer her struggles to further her literary career and the overwhelming chores she endured as a wife and mother. In March 1897 she wrote to Cottman informing him that she was unable to commit to being on the program for the annual convention of the Western Association of Writers. She had attended one of the literary group's meetings in the past, but indicated there were "several disagreeable results to my becoming a member." Strauss failed to relate the "disagreeable results" to Cottman and lamented that her responsibilities as a homemaker meant that she could never "go any place that I want to go, or do anything that I really want to." She also had "so very many cares and so much hard work to do that I can find little time for writing," Strauss confided to Cottman. Because of hard economic times, a Chicago newspaper for which she had been doing some work at a small salary had laid her off and she saw no chance of being hired again. "The loss of this salary threw me back in to the kitchen again and, though I have a great fondness for the kitchen and think it is not half a bad place to be," Strauss said, "I am unable to *make* much progress in literature." Although the *Rockville Tribune* columnist related to Cottman that she thought she possessed "talent—and not genius," being unable to utilize fully her writing skills often became too much for Strauss to bear. It made her sick, she said, to "see others who have scarcely a grain of talent printing their trash in respectable publications."[20]

In spite of her complaints to Cottman, Strauss, by the turn of the century, was more and more successful with her writing, publishing sketches, short stories, and essays in several publications, including the *Woman's Home Companion*, the *Horse Review of Chicago* (edited by Strauss's childhood friend Homer Kline), and the *Indianapolis News*. Her pleasure at her literary accomplishments, however, was dampened by tragedy in her personal life. Strauss's mother, who had been a constant source of support, died on 7 January 1903, which also marked Strauss's fortieth birthday. Susan Humphries's death came after an almost supernatural incident involving Strauss. A few days before her death, Susan Humphries, who was at her daughter Betty's home, became ill. Keeping watch over her mother one cold, clear night, Strauss heard singing—first a single voice and then what sounded like a choir—coming from somewhere in the house. There was a handyman employed by her sister to tend the furnace and, at first, Strauss thought it was him singing. The handyman, however, could not be found in the house and there was nobody on the street in front of the home. "She stood transfixed for a moment," Strauss's granddaughter, Juliet Snowden, related, "then entered the sickroom as the strains of music gradually died away. In the dimly lit room she looked at her mother and saw at once that a sinister change had occurred." Humphries died shortly after the incident.[21]

With her grandmother's death, her mother's life changed, particularly her writing, according to Marcia Strouse. "Out of her grief came a greater conception of other's pain and the fruit of her sorrow was the sympathy which endeared her so closely to her readers," she noted, adding that her mother's "best work" came after Susan Humphries died. Also, with her mother's friends growing older,

Strauss spent more time "absorbed with her work," her daughter said. Although Marcia Strouse had many happy memories of her mother since her grandmother's death, the "old hilarious days never quite came back."[22]

Her personal loss came during a year that saw Strauss achieve the biggest success ever in her writing life. For some time Strauss had signed her articles as The Country Contributor, a name suggested to her by her husband. One of her articles submitted to the *Indianapolis News*, an essay on the month of April, caught the particular attention of the newspaper's editor-in-chief, Charles R. Williams, who wrote her a letter complimenting her on her work. "I was scared and pleased to death," Strauss said of Williams's letter and subsequent offer of a regular column in the newspaper.[23] On 21 November 1903 a new column, signed The Country Contributor, made its debut in the *Indianapolis News*. Strauss's column became a mainstay of the newspaper's Saturday edition, appearing there each week for the next fifteen years. The *Indianapolis News* had had its eye on Strauss for some time. Just that past August, the newspaper featured an article on Strauss titled "Talented Writer at Home in Rockville." The piece, written by a staff correspondent and featuring a photo of Strauss, noted that the Rockville native's work had captured for itself "many readers of the class that appreciate choice English and delicate distinctions."[24]

The decision by the *Indianapolis News* to offer Strauss a place for her views may also have been prompted by financial considerations. At the turn of the century, newspapers throughout the country placed a greater emphasis on appealing to female readers, not, as one journalism historian notes, due to the emancipation of the sex, but rather "mainly to the growth of department-store advertising," which was directed toward women in the home. In addition to special women's sections, newspapers brought onto their staffs more female reporters.[25] More than a year before Strauss's column began appearing in the *Indianapolis News*, Hilton U. Brown, the newspaper's general manager, wrote to his boss, owner Delavan Smith, that he had instructed the editorial department to "keep it as a perpetual assignment to secure stuff of interest to households and women, but not necessarily stuff that is to be labeled womens reading."[26] Also, with approximately half of the *Indianapolis News*'s circulation coming from outside Indianapolis and its suburbs, the newspaper needed copy that could attract rural readers from throughout the state.[27]

In finding a home for her writing at the *Indianapolis News*, Strauss joined a newspaper considered by many as the "best-written and best-edited" of its time.[28] The city's oldest newspaper, the "Great Hoosier Daily" had its start in 1869 under the ownership of John H. Holliday, who operated the daily afternoon newspaper as a politically independent institution. In 1892 Holliday, in ill health, sold the newspaper to Ohio native and former Associated Press manager William Henry Smith. Smith managed the newspaper with the assistance of his son Delavan, who inherited the *Indianapolis News* upon his father's death in 1896, and his son-in-law Williams (United States senator and vice president Charles W. Fairbanks was also a silent partner in the operation). One element of the newspaper's success, according to Indiana historian Jacob Piatt Dunn Jr., was its habit of hiring the best writers for every department. Whenever anyone showed ability on a rival newspaper, said Dunn, also a veteran Indianapolis journalist, the *Indianapolis News* "went after him and usually got him without trouble, for some newspaper men prefer day work."[29]

The reporters and editors hired by the *Indianapolis News* included such luminaries as Brown, Louis Howland, and Meredith Nicholson. When Strauss's column appeared in 1903, the newspaper had also been publishing for some years the drawings of Frank McKinney "Kin" Hubbard who, in 1904, created the cracker-barrel philosopher Abe Martin of Brown County, Indiana, whose *bon mots* like "it's no disgrace t' be poor, but it might as well be" and "when a feller says, 'It hain't th' money, but th' principle o' th' thing,' it's the money," drew national acclaim. Hubbard worked in a section of the newspaper dubbed the "Idle Ward." In addition to Hubbard, other members of that delightful company included ace reporter William Herschell and cartoonist Gaar Williams. The trio was productive, but to others at the paper they seemed "idle because they always had time for talk."[30]

Strauss's early columns for the *Indianapolis News* set the tone for her subsequent work for the newspaper. Her writings related to readers some background on the author, including her early poverty-filled days as a young girl growing up in Rockville and subsequent life as a wife and mother at her home, dubbed "Grouch Place." Interwoven with her autobiography was her emphasis on the worth and value of the simple life over that of society. "Life has so many better things to offer," Strauss said, "that the greatest pity of all seems to me to be for people who care most for hats and gowns, chairs and rugs and all the soulless things made by man. Nothing is quite so common as style. Nothing so tiresome as mere etiquette, nothing so nauseating as the round of stupid gatherings we call society, and nothing so execrable as what women like to call culture."[31] Instead of attending a temperance meeting, church social, or other society function, Strauss emphasized to women the importance and honor of serving as a homemaker, even comparing cooking a meal for her family to a religious duty. "Why can not women know," she wondered, "that good cooking is a means of grace, that there is spirit in it, that in preparing a good meal we are making soul nourishment for our loved ones. And again, why can not women know that cooking is an accomplishment, a fine art, an acquirement of which any one may well be proud?"[32]

The "simple, personal, and sincere style" utilized by Strauss in her writings made her column a hit with *Indianapolis News* readers, who wrote countless letters to the newspaper seeking more information on The Country Contributor.[33] In response to its readers' requests, the newspaper sent its feature reporter, Herschell, to Rockville to glean more information on its budding star columnist. Born in Spencer, Indiana, the son of Scottish immigrants, Herschell left school in the seventh grade to work in a machine shop, but gradually gravitated to a career in journalism. He worked for the *Huntingburg Independent* and *Princeton News* before joining the *Indianapolis News* staff in 1902. In traveling to Rockville, Herschell, who also contributed verse to the newspaper, attempted in his article on Strauss to answer such questions from readers as: "Is she sincere? Does she really mean what she says? Is there such a place as 'Grouch Place'? Does she live the life she writes about?" The answer, the *Indianapolis News* reporter said, was an enthusiastic "You bet!"[34]

The article, which appeared above Strauss's regular column for the week, included a number of photographs depicting Strauss and her home, described by Herschell as a good-sized, comfortable-looking house located on a Rockville side street (514 N. College). Originally home to the Beadle family, the Strauss family moved into the house in 1893. Dubbed its unusual name by a family member, Grouch Place was so named, according to Strauss, because her family had "an ancient habit of having things out with each other at once and discarding all perfunctory amenities. We never get very savage and we never harbor a secret grievance."[35] Herschell, upon meeting Strauss for the first time, characterized her as being "of medium in hight [*sic*], slender, and of the type called blonde. She is alert and possessed of a disposition that sees things on the sunny side of the fence." The home itself, he said, was not elaborately furnished, but "every nook of it breathes of comfort and happiness." At the rear of the house stood a chicken yard and garden. A continuous flower bed ringed the house and old-fashioned rose bushes filled the yard. "There is no affectation in any member of the Strouse-Strauss family," the reporter wrote. "They are what they are, and this is a worthy state."[36]

Before taking Herschell on a horse-drawn tour of Rockville, Strauss related to the reporter her method of writing. Noticing a small sewing table in the living room on which were an ink bottle, two pens, and a writing tablet, Herschell asked her if that was where she worked. "I use it [the table] most of the time," Strauss responded. "Frequently I pile into a big rocking-chair and write with the tablet on my knee. Another time I open the little writing desk there in the corner and scribble at it for awhile. It is all as the notion excites me." Her doctrine, she added, consisted of getting happy and staying that way. "When trouble comes meet it," she told Herschell, "get along with it as best you can, and then let loose of it. I like to have fun, to play cards occasionally and go to a party now and then. I'm not much of a club woman and only a fair Presbyterian. Otherwise I'm all right."[37]

Just two years after establishing herself as a mainstay in one of Indiana's best newspapers, Strauss and her writing—the "simple sincere stuff that I had thought out and worked out all by myself" as Strauss called her work—caught the attention of a man who would introduce the Rockville native to the rest of the country: Edward Bok, *Ladies' Home Journal* editor. Her ability to take the "commoner things of the plain, simple life of a people not sated with over-indulgence . . . and discussing these in a bright, sparkling style" proved to be just what Bok needed for the pages of a magazine that became the first in the nation to reach a million readers.[38] Strauss and her philosophy provided a perfect fit for a man whose idea was to "keep women in the home especially as there are enough writers who are trying to take her out of it."[39]

Notes

[1] "Squibs and Sayings," *Rockville Tribune*, 9 February 1893.

[2] "Death and Funeral of Mrs. Isaac R. Strouse, the Well Known 'County Contributor,'" *Rockville Republican*, 29 May 1918.

[3] Strouse, "Reminiscences About Life of Country Contributor," *Indianapolis News*, 5 June 1926.

[4] "Squibs and Sayings," *Rockville Tribune*, 4 May 1893.

[5] "Squibs and Sayings," *Rockville Tribune*, 11 May 1893.

[6] Strouse, "Reminiscences About Life of Country Contributor," *Indianapolis News*, 5 June 1926.

[7] "Squibs and Sayings," *Rockville Tribune*, 13 April 1893.

[8] Some of the first literary organizations founded in the state were the Indianapolis Literary Club in 1877, the Terre Haute Literary Club in 1881, the Ouiatenon Club (Crawfordsville) in 1883, and the Western Association of Writers (dubbed the "Literary Gravel Pit Association" by its critics) in 1886. See, Phillips, *Indiana in Transition*, 504–5; Shumaker, *A History of Indiana Literature*, 12–14; and Ray Boomhower, "Prologue," in Barbara Olenyik Morrow, *From Ben–Hur to Sister Carrie: Remembering the Lives and Works of Five Indiana Authors* (Indianapolis: Guild Press of Indiana, Inc., 1995).

[9] Strouse, "Reminiscences About Life of Country Contributor," *Indianapolis News*, 22 May 1926.

[10] "Audi Alteram Partem," *Rockville Republican*, 19 April 1893.

[11] Strouse, "Reminiscences About Life of Country Contributor," *Indianapolis News*, 5 June 1926.

[12] "Squibs and Sayings," *Rockville Tribune*, 22 April 1908.

[13] George S. Cottman, "An Autobiography," *Indiana Magazine of History* 31 (June 1935): 133.

[14] See Strouse, "Reminiscences About Life of Country Contributor," *Indianapolis News*, 22 May 1926.

[15] Harriet Adams Sawyer, "The Western Association of Writers: Some Impressions Received at its Recent Convention held at Dayton, Ohio," *The Chaperone* 8 (August 1892): 434. See also, Cottman, "The Western Asso-

ciation of Writers: A Literary Reminiscence," *Indiana Magazine of History* 29 (September 1933): 187–97. A regular attendee at the WAW's annual gatherings, Cottman also joined a subset of the group called "Ye Owl Club," the function of which was to "recuperate its members after the severe celebrations of the day" with sessions beginning late at night. Led by the Most Grand Hoo! Hoo!, the club's members, which set dues at one cent a year, had to be ready, whenever the Most Grand Hoo! Hoo! commanded, to contribute "an impromptu song, story, recitation, hoot or other recuperative diversion." Cottman, "The Western Association of Writers," 196–97. For more on Cottman's life, see Cottman, "An Autobiography," and Ray Boomhower, "'Devoted to the Past for the Sake of the Present': George S. Cottman and the *Indiana Magazine of History*," *Indiana Magazine of History* 93 (March 1997): 1–17.

[16] Juliet V. Strauss to George S. Cottman, 18 September 1896, George S. Cottman Papers, Indiana Division, Indiana State Library, Indianapolis.

[17] Cottman to Strauss, 23 September 1896, Cottman Papers, ISL.

[18] Ibid.

[19] Strauss to Cottman, 2 October 1896, Cottman Papers, ISL.

[20] Strauss to Cottman, 4 March 1897, Cottman Papers, ISL.

[21] Juliet Snowden, *Legends and Lore of Parke County, Indiana* (n.p., 1967), 27.

[22] Ott, "Some Memories of My Mother," *Rockville Tribune Memorial Supplement*, 4 June 1918.

[23] Strouse, "Reminiscences About Life of Country Contributor," *Indianapolis News*, 5 June 1926.

[24] "Talented Writer at Home in Rockville," *Indianapolis News*, 29 August 1903. See also, Strouse, "Reminiscences About Life of Country Contributor," *Indianapolis News*, 5 June 1926, and "Reminiscence," *Rockville Tribune Memorial Supplement*, 4 June 1918.

[25] Mott, *American Journalism*, 599.

[26] Hilton U. Brown to Delavan Smith, 22 May 1902, Delavan Smith Papers, Indiana Historical Society, Indianapolis.

[27] In the first quarter of 1903, the *Indianapolis News's* circulation stood at 73,168. Of that number, 37,990 resided in Indianapolis and its suburbs. Advertising managers at the newspaper boasted to potential advertisers that the *Indianapolis News* reached each of Indiana's ninety-two counties. See, *Indianapolis News* rate card, 18 April 1903, Delavan Smith Papers, IHS.

²⁸ Phillips, *Indiana in Transition*, 528. Charles Arthur Carlisle, purchasing agent for Studebaker Brothers Manufacturing Company in South Bend, Indiana, went so far as to write an *Indianapolis News* advertising executive that he wished someone from the Indianapolis newspaper "would come out here and establish a first class daily in the city of South Bend. We need one just like the 'Indianapolis News.'" Charles Arthur Carlisle to M. Lee Starke, 23 February 1904, Delavan Smith Papers, IHS.

²⁹ Jacob Piatt Dunn Jr., *Greater Indianapolis: The History, the Industries, the Institutions, and the People of a City of Homes*, 2 vols. (Chicago: The Lewis Publishing Co., 1910), 1:401. For the history of the *Indianapolis News*, see also Hilton U. Brown, *A Book of Memories* (Indianapolis: Butler University, 1951); Phillips, *Indiana in Transition*, 528–29; Miller, *Indiana Newspaper Bibliography*, 281; and Beth Murphy, "Indianapolis News" in David J. Bodenhamer and Robert G. Barrows, eds., *The Encyclopedia of Indianapolis* (Bloomington and Indianapolis: Indiana University Press, 1994), 796–97.

³⁰ Fred C. Kelly, *The Life and Times of Kin Hubbard, Creator of Abe Martin* (New York: Farrar, Straus, and Young, 1952), 92. Herschell had fond memories of his days at the *Indianapolis News* with Hubbard. He recalled one incident when Hubbard, a devoted fan of perennial Democratic presidential candidate William Jennings Bryan, took his hero's last defeat in stride. Ducking into a darkroom at the newspaper's offices after Bryan's campaign went down in flames, Hubbard soon appeared swathed head to foot in bandages and supported by crutches. Herschell noted that his friend "limped through the editorial rooms. He neither smiled nor spoke, but went on his battered way, the rest of us roaring our delight at his satire." Ray Boomhower, "A 'Dapper Dan with the Soul of an Imp': Kin Hubbard, Creator of Abe Martin," *Traces of Indiana and Midwestern History* 5 (fall 1993):44–45. For more information on Hubbard's life and career, see also David S. Hawes, ed., *The Best of Kin Hubbard: Abe Martin's Sayings and Wisecracks, Abe's Neighbors, His Almanack, Comic Drawings* (Bloomington: Indiana University Press, 1984).

³¹ "The Short and Simple Annals of the Poor," *Indianapolis News*, 21 November 1903.

³² "Housekeeping No Penance," *Indianapolis News*, 28 November 1903.

³³ Shumaker, *A History of Indiana Literature*, 493. In his book on Hoosier writing, Shumaker placed Strauss and her work within the "Fa-

miliar Essay" category, as opposed to the more formal or serious essay. The familiar essay, he said, is "usually more personal, somewhat whimsical, and of a lighter touch than the formal essay; yet, the familiar essay may still embody a serious purpose." Shumaker placed Meredith Nicholson and Booth Tarkington as the leading familiar essay writers in the golden age, with Strauss, John Tarkington (Booth Tarkington's father), and Louis Howland, an *Indianapolis News* reporter, on a lower tier. Ibid., 489–91.

[34] "Who is the Country Contributor? What is She Really Like? Some Frequently Asked Questions Answered After a Visit to Her Home," *Indianapolis News*, 5 May 1906. For more on Herschell's life, see Ray Boomhower, "William Herschell," *Encyclopedia of Indianapolis*, 671; Brown, *A Book of Memories*, 221–23; and Shumaker, *A History of Indiana Literature*, 256–57.

[35] "A Plain Country Woman's Christmas Ideas," *Ladies' Home Journal*, December 1906.

[36] "Who is the Country Contributor?" *Indianapolis News*, 5 May 1906.

[37] Ibid.

[38] "Our Best Known Citizen," *Rockville Republican*, 29 May 1918.

[39] Salme Harju Steinberg, *Reformer in the Marketplace: Edward W. Bok and* The Ladies' Home Journal (Baton Rouge: Louisiana State University Press, 1979), 66.

The Ideas of a Plain Country Woman

DRAWN BY LAETITIA HERR

THE month of May is typified in my early recollections by a washing-day at grandmother's. There was a pungent odor of cleanliness about the place exhaling from the lye-soap in the big gourd, and the walk from the kitchen door to the milkhouse was scoured to a rich cream color. The cinnamon rose-bush was in bloom, and the dazzling whiteness of the clothes on the line as they flapped against the deep blue sky, together with the long stretch of green, green grass that felt so good to one's bare feet, made a combination of vivid coloring that hurt the eyes and made one wish to look away across the orchard, where there was a soft pink and white mist, to the woods, traced delicately in their early verdure.

Grandmother, Resting on the Bench under the big sycamore tree, her arms bare and her hands pink and crinkled from long immersion in the suds, took me on her knee and told me about the laurel that must be blooming in the mountains far away where her old home was. She said that no flower that blooms out here in this strange country can ever be so pretty as the mountain laurel, not even the cinnamon rose which I admired so much, or the May pinks down in the garden, freshly uncovered from their winter sleep and mingling their perfume with the scent of upturned earth from the garden beds and cool, new paths, where it was an awesome delight to go pattering at twilight. The garden was a new world rediscovered, and all through the summer it would have its moods for us—its remoteness of sweet corn and pole-beans, its aristocratic retirements of sage and musk geranium and lavender, and far in one corner its melancholy patch of hemp which grandmother raised, partly for seed for the canary, partly to remind her of the hempfields she used to know in Old Virginia.

The Big, Gray Farmhouse was sweet from top to bottom with the rejuvenation of spring. The girthing-striped rag carpet which grandmother had woven was freshly laid over clean straw on the sitting-room floor. The sprigged muslin curtains at the parlor windows were beautifully laundered; the quilts had all been upon the line, washed or aired as was needed. They made a goodly array, filling up every available inch of line and running over upon the garden paling. Those on the paling were decidedly below the salt, plebeian nine-patch or four-patch. The aristocrats on the line had nothing to do with them. There was the Whig rose, the star pattern, the Irish chain, the ocean wave, the log cabin and other patterns whose names I have forgotten, besides the "tufted" counterpanes and spreads that great-grandmother had woven.

Grandmother must have been very tired indeed that day, but she did not say so; she only told me about the laurel, and I remembered it.

I think it was from the blood of Old Virginia that I inherited the crude feeling for life that has been such a treasure to me through years which some people might call hard.

Among the People of my blood who lived amid the green hills and blue mountains of the Shenandoah Valley there flourished the true type of the simple life. Charles Wagner failed to elucidate the simple life to the mind of the wayfaring man. The Scripture, as usual, hits the mark when it insinuates that the wayfaring man is likely to be a fool. He is, and his manner of "faring" doesn't indicate anything. He may be tramping, or riding in his automobile or his private car.

These valley people lived very heartily to the day and hour. They relished life. They were not trying to do anything but live. The old walls that had sheltered their ancestors were devoid of ornament, the bare floors were polished by the feet of generations, the staunch old furniture was mellow with the tones of age. Fires in huge chimneys were dully smouldering or springing to welcome beckonings at nightfall. There was no effort toward elegance. The people were the home. If you have ever known the air of such a place style and interior decoration will always seem cheap to you. It was what they lacked that made them fine.

I Hope the Reader will not take this as an epigram. I detest epigrams, and they have been so fashionable of late years. Our popular fiction has bristled with the covert immorality of smart sayings.

When I say that it is what we lack that makes us fine I mean that Life stands ever ready with her compensations for all of our losses.

I love that stanza of Mrs. Browning's:

"In the pleasant orchard-closes
'God bless all our gains!' say we;
But 'May God bless all our losses!'
Better suits with our degree."

From these simple-hearted people, who lived so close to "wind and sun and summer rain," I inherited God's best blessing for all our losses—a keen taste for living.

It was on a fourteenth of May—I remember the plum tree was in bloom, and the moonlight flooded our little village dooryard—when the boy and I vowed to marry as soon as we were rich enough. Later we decided to do it anyway and not wait to be rich enough. It was a dreadful mistake, as we found out later when there were some children with nobody but us to look after them. Man remains a child long after woman has come to a realizing sense of duty. My young husband—a Tom Sawyer village lad—had little taste for the ties of domesticity.

There are Two Distinct Kinds of Men: domestic men and the other kind. The latter are pretty sure to be attractive to girls. They are likely to ride horses and carry guns and have dogs following them.

I always wondered what became of the girl who ran away with Young Lochinvar. I warrant the quiet fellow who stood awkwardly by and let his bride be carried away would have made the better husband. "A laggard in love and a dastard in war" is sure to be a good hand to do up the chores and dry the dishes and stay at home evenings. He will go to church with his wife, and set the hens, and run the clothes through the wringer, and read aloud from the farm paper while she fashions garments for the little ones from the worn-out raiment of their elders. This is the domestic kind.

At the risk of seeming unduly personal I may remark that my life-partner was the other kind. He was a sportsman, a man of the streets and town, a man's man in every sense of the word—and I was a mother, a child in years, but I had a world to make for my children, a castle to build—and how was I to build it unless I learned to make bricks without straw?

In Former Articles I have spoken to women of the duty and pleasure of work; let me now remind them of the pleasure and duty of idleness. If I had not known how to loaf and when to be a vagabond I should have fallen by the wayside, or have grown old and hard-featured and bitter, with no relish for life and no heart for song and story.

I know that city people believe they have all the advantages, but I am sure that country-town people are the lords of the earth when it comes to good living.

No matter how poor we are we are always in reach of luxuries. A clear fire, a fresh egg, a pitcher of sweet milk or of pure water—these may seem very unimportant things to the woman who wishes to broaden her life by moving to a city, but you narrow your life immensely when you dispense with anything sweet and natural that goes to sustain it.

My Instincts were Sharpened to the bodily needs of my children. I was like a tiger-mother when she says to Life: "Give me something for those little cubs!" And I got it, because Life always obeys when you speak to her like that.

But there was so much more besides food to be found for them. There was beauty and the joy of living, and the charm of world-lore, and the realm of the imaginary. Many mothers more fortunately situated than I was cannot find time to convey these things to their children. They have too many "interests."

I did heartily covet the grille-work and draperies that adorned my friends' houses, but while they were busy cleaning them I found time to lie on the old faded lounge in our little library and read Shakespeare or Poe, or go roaming off with the children to hunt spring flowers.

We were always too poor to keep a horse, but we kept one. You are up in the world when you own a horse, and if you have a dog you are sure of at least one faithful henchman for retinue. My children and I with our horse and dog made many triumphal pilgrimages through the world of May. I think our rank in the court of spring was fairly high, at least we never found any lack of welcome there, and always came home garlanded and loaded with favors.

My Friends Thought I was atoning for my mistakes by making more. They felt I was not diligent enough and was inculcating in my children habits of idleness.

Many of my friends had no children and were fairly insolent in their triumph over it, but they know now that I lived in the sunshine of life while they toiled dully in the shadow.

I wish I could impress upon women some understanding of the value of many things they are taught to discard. The great trouble with women is that they are all trying to follow the same lifeless model. In their passion for refinement they lose the very essence of life; and in doing so they often fling man back upon immorality, in his natural seeking for the primitive. Man instinctively reaches out for the primal mate—and too often she is not there.

I Heartily Pity Women who have lived in the narrow groove of ladyhood. Some people may consider me coarse. It is true, my hands are not nice and I do laugh heartily, and perhaps I do not "appear" quite well in fashionable society; but I believe the word coarse is as often misused as any in the language. It seems to me that nothing coarsens a woman like luxury.

Some months ago I was dining at a fashionable hotel in a city when a couple entered the room and sat down at an adjoining table. They were people who "lived" at the hotel. I saw at once that they belonged to the "fortunate" class—one could tell by the cut of their clothes, the diamond rings that fairly stiffened the woman's pudgy fingers, the man's air of deadly boredom, and the woman's hostile countenance. She bestowed a casual ferocity on my old-fashioned sleeves out of the supply of scorn she seemed to carry on hand. The puffy circles under her eyes and the unwholesome stoutness of her figure betokened the stupid ease of the woman who "doesn't have to work."

There was some terrapin on the bill-of-fare—I think it was not genuine—and the couple discussed its merits in the dead-alive fashion common to the rich man and his wife, who are astute with the fashionable necessity of expurgating from their conversation any hint of originality or possible interest.

I did wish I could tell them about the time I killed the turtle, and how much better it was than what they were eating.

My Husband Has a Habit of bringing home his minnow bucket and leaving it on the back porch for me to explore after supper is over and he has flown to town with its cheerful freedom from domestic cares. Whatever I find there is mine to do as I like with, be it an eel, a bullfrog or a mess of pretty black bass. Many a spring evening has found me in the back lot taking the scales off the fish while the children danced about in impatience for the bladders to sail for boats, and the cats contested claims for the heads. This time it was a great big turtle—and it was alive. I shut the children and cats up in the kitchen and gave my undivided attention to the turtle, for I had never dressed one before.

The fat woman with the rings would have fainted dead away if she had seen me dispatch that turtle and split its shell open with the hatchet. But I knew how real terrapin tasted and she did not, and as I observed her I suddenly knew that there were such a lot of things that I knew which she did not, and I was glad of it!

In Reviewing a Period of My Life which is closed now, since the children are gone away, I am conscious of a distinct charm in the living of it, with all its hardships and heartaches.

I believe I can tell women what that charm was and that they may profit by it. It was variety. Whenever it was possible I submitted to the mood. I kept up an armed neutrality with Duty and never allowed her to get the better of me. I never followed anybody's lead. I lived my own life. If I wished to ride a horse, or to play a game, or to go wading in the creek with the children I always did it.

I never strained my eyesight or racked my nerves trying to arrive at small perfections. I avoided rivalries and emulations. In short, I lived.

The Other Evening the Boy—he is forty-six years old now and has scarcely a wrinkle on his face—hung up his hat and coat and sat down to spend the evening at home. It was chilly and I had started a little fire on the hearth. We looked at each other, and the tears sprang up in our eyes because the children are gone—and because——

I felt like quoting these lines to him—but I didn't:

"When all the world is old, lad,
And all the trees are brown;
And all the sport is stale, lad,
And all the wheels run down:
Creep home, and take your place there,
The spent and maimed among:
God grant you find one face there
You loved when all was young."

The Country Contributor

Chapter Four
The Simple Life

For Edward W. Bok, editor of the *Ladies' Home Journal*, America's leading woman's magazine at the turn of the century, the secret to his periodical's success was simple: find writing talent and publish it. In describing his technique to a reporter for the *New York Sun*, Bok, a poor Dutch immigrant who found success in the United States, gave as an example a column he had first noticed in an Indianapolis newspaper [the *Indianapolis News*]. "It struck me as well done. I watched it for some time. Then I took pains to find out who wrote it," Bok told the reporter. He discovered that the writer was "a woman in a tiny out-of-the-way town in Indiana." After a favorable report from one of his staff, who traveled to the Hoosier state to visit the woman, Bok "made her an offer to do some work for us," which led to a regular column in the *Journal* titled "The Ideas of a Plain Country Woman."[1]

The woman Bok described to the New York journalist was Strauss. From its first appearance in the *Journal* in November 1905, the Rockville native's writing proved to be a hit with the magazine's readers. In just a little over a year, the *Journal*'s editors declared that Strauss's efforts, usually two columns in length illustrated with bucolic images and signed simply with her nom de plume "The Country Contributor," had "become one of the most successful departments *The Journal* has ever published."[2] The national woman's magazine also accepted a variety of Strauss's other work, including an autobiographical series titled "The Chronicles of a Queer Girl," which ran in consecutive issues from June to December 1907, and the two-part short story "A Girl in Old Viginia: The Romantic Larks of a Girl in the

Old Romantic Days," which appeared in the *Journal* in April 1911. Both pieces were lavishly illustrated and published under Strauss's own name. Most importantly for the Rockville native, her work for the magazine drew enough attention that a book of her columns and some new essays was published as *The Ideas of a Plain Country Woman* in 1908.

The editor who brought Strauss such prominence was a man who had supreme confidence in his abilities to make the *Journal* the authoritative voice for American women in the early twentieth century; after all, he had started life as a poor immigrant only to rise to become one of America's best-known men—a Horatio Alger story come to life. Edward William Bok was born in the Dutch seaport town of den Helder, the second son born to a well-respected family. The Bok family, however, fell on hard financial times and immigrated to America in 1870, settling in Brooklyn. Bok left school at age thirteen to take a job as an office boy for the Western Union Telegraph Company. "I never went to school again," he recalled. "I have hustled from that time until now." In 1882, he became a stenographer for the publishing firm Henry Holt & Company, leaving two years later to join Charles Scribner's Sons. Starting his own periodical, *Brooklyn Magazine*, in 1884, Bok later created his own syndicate, the Bok Syndicate Press, supplying newspapers with literary features and material on and for women.[3]

Bok won national fame, however, for editing a monthly woman's magazine first started by Cyrus Curtis of Philadelphia as a column called "Women and Home" in his four-page weekly, the *Tribune and the Farmer*. His wife, Louisa Knapp Curtis, was unimpressed by her husband's efforts, telling him, "I don't mean to make fun of you, but if you really knew how funny this material sounds to a woman, you would laugh too."[4] Turning the department over to his wife, it soon proved so popular that the Curtises issued a monthly supplement for women in the weekly *Tribune*. The first issue of the *Ladies' Home Journal and Practical Housekeeper* appeared in December 1883. The *Ladies' Home Journal* was just one of a number of periodicals devoted to women readers, who became an important portion of the reading public in the nineteenth century. Such journals had begun appearing as early as the 1790s, but their numbers quickly rose with the explosive growth of magazine publishing that took place from 1825 to 1860. Popular women's magazines of the day, which targeted mainly a well-to-do audience, included *Godey's Lady Book* (dubbed the *Vogue* of its era), *Graham's Magazine*, and *Peterson's Magazine*. None of these publications, however, matched the success enjoyed by the *Ladies' Home Journal*, which grew to have 488,000 readers by 1889—an "incredible figure" for a periodical at that time.[5]

The *Journal's* success, paradoxically, led to Louisa Knapp Curtis's resignation as editor. Her thirteen-year-old daughter, Mary Louise Curtis (who married Bok on 22 October 1896), complained that whenever she wanted her mother's attention she always seemed to be busy with her editorial duties. With his wife's decision to relinquish her editorship, Cyrus Curtis asked Bok to take over. In agreeing to accept the editor's job, Bok knew that he possessed no special understanding about women and their needs and expressed no desire "to know them [women] better or to seek to understand them," adding that as a man he could not, no matter how much an effort he made, succeed in such an attempt. Bok did, however, understand the needs of a home. "He had always lived in one," he noted in his autobiography (written entirely in third person), "had struggled to keep it together, and he knew every inch of the hard road that makes for domestic permanence amid adverse financial considerations. And at the home he aimed rather than at the woman in it." He also possessed a firm vision for the magazine. In his Pulitzer Prize–winning autobiography, he said that he wanted the *Journal* to be an "authoritative clearing-house for all the problems confronting a woman in the home, that brought itself closely into contact with these problems and tried to solve them in an entertaining and efficient way; and yet a magazine of uplift and inspiration: a magazine, in other words, that would give light and leading in the woman's world."[6]

On 20 October 1889 Bok assumed his duties as the magazine's

editor. As a twenty-six-year-old bachelor who had just become a highly paid editor of one of the country's leading magazines for women, Bok instantly became a favorite figure of fun with America's press, which filled its columns with jokes and puns about the Dutch immigrant. This situation, however, fit in perfectly with Bok's plans to put aside the usually impersonal nature of being a magazine editor. "He felt the time had come . . . for the editor of some magazine to project his personality through the printed page," he noted, "and to convince the public that he was not an oracle removed from the people, but a real human being who could talk and not merely write on paper."[7] Unlike other magazines of the time period, the *Journal*, Bok said, would not make the "grievous mistake" of writing down to the public or merely "'giving the public what it wants.'" Instead, Bok and the magazine gave its subscribers "the subjects they asked for, but invariably on a slightly higher plane; and each year he raised the standard a notch." The American public, Bok reasoned, always "wants something a little better than it asks for, and the successful man, in catering to it, is he who follows this golden rule."[8] He strove to make the magazine appeal to the "intelligent American woman rather than the intellectual type," the burgeoning middle-class audience hungry for reading matter that appealed to its interests.[9]

In following his "golden rule" Bok brought to the *Journal*'s pages some of the finest writers of the time including William Dean Howells, Rudyard Kipling, Bret Harte, and Mark Twain. Bok also offered prizes to the magazine's readers for the best suggestions offered as to the *Journal*'s contents and used their ideas to create departments to advise women such as "Side Talks to Girls" with Ruth Ashmore (a task handled at first by Bok himself). He continued his predecessor's policy of seeking and responding to correspondence from the magazine's readers and charged his employees with answering every letter "quickly, fully, and courteously, with the questioner always encouraged to come again if any problem of whatever nature came to her."[10]. Bok's policy paid off; in the last four months of 1912 alone, the magazine received ninety-seven thousand letters. To ensure that his wishes about responding promptly to correspondence were being followed, every six months Bok wrote a letter to his magazine under an assumed name to each department and monitored the responses he received, praising good work and criticizing severely those who failed in their duties.[11]

Like his friend President Theodore Roosevelt, Bok used his "bully pulpit" to promote numerous reforms. He used the *Journal's* pages to campaign for outlawing the public drinking cup (which promoted disease), eliminating billboards as a way of beautifying communities, simplifying American home design, preserving the country's natural areas, and promoting more open discussion on the previously taboo subject of venereal disease. The magazine's greatest reform achievement came in 1892 when Bok announced that the *Journal* would no longer accept patent-medicine advertisements. Over the next few years, Bok used his power as editor to call upon his readers to stop using patent medicines and, in 1906, was a strong voice in favor of the Pure Food and Drug Act. No less an authority than historian Louis Filler, in his history of the "muckrakers"—journalists and writers like Upton Sinclair and Ida Tarbell who urged Americans to reform industry and its unsafe practices—said that Bok's *Journal* challenged its readers by emphasizing in its pages some of the day's most important issues. "Its greatest significance for our history, however," said Filler, "lies in the fact that it was one of those publications that, by broadening the circle of popular-magazine readers, prepared the way for the muckrakers."[12]

Despite his reforming instincts, Bok, and consequently the *Journal*, maintained a conservative view about a woman's place in society. As a "steadying influence" in American life, a woman, according to Bok, belonged in the home living a simple life and improving her family through her moral power because a female was "better, purer, conscientious and morally stronger."[13] Bok used his position as *Journal* editor to criticize what he saw as the superficiality of women's clubs and came out against giving women the right to vote because he believed that American women "were not ready to exercise the privilege intelligently and that their mental attitude was against it."[14] Although he did print an article in 1910 by Jane Addams of Hull House fame outlining the reasons why women should vote, Bok's own view closely followed that of former president Grover Cleveland who, five years before Addams's article, stated in the *Journal* that allowing women the right to suffrage would disrupt "a natural equilibrium so nicely adjusted to the attributes and limitations of both [women and men] that it cannot be disturbed without social confusion and peril."[15]

What Bok wanted for women, and all people, was a philosophy inspired by the writings of Charles Wagner, a French minister and author of the book *The Simple Life*, published in 1901. Influnced by Wagner, Bok emphasized an easy way to happiness through the simple life, which included the following: "Make home happy; hold loved ones first in your heart; leave off fussing over fashionable ways of living; be natural, and you will be living the simple life though you ride in a motorcar, clean house by electricity, entertain at the country club, and have every convenience known to man. The quality of the individual is what determines the simple life, never his surroundings."[16]

Because of Bok's belief in the necessity for a simple life, and the traditional role for a woman in that life, it is not surprising that Strauss's writing drew his attention. After all, the Rockville native had been expressing these same ideas for years in her work for the *Rockville Tribune* and *Indianapolis News*. From her first column for the *Journal* in November 1905 and for years thereafter, Strauss continued to emphasize these same ideals and also promoted the value and spiritual worth of being a homemaker. Like Bok, she attempted through her writing to convince women that their proper sphere was not as wage earners, but inside the home. "I should like it, if it were possible, to inspire my sex . . . with the idea that theirs is a great big responsible job, and that the women who get out of it are only those who are not big enough to undertake it," Strauss said. The woman who managed to make a comfortable and pleasant home for her family even when the "weather is bad and finances low and everything and everybody jaded with the wear and tear of life, is a genius, and there are many such in the world." To those who called upon women to look beyond the home and go out in the working world, Strauss argued that there was only one thing more important "than to go where you are needed, and that is to stay where you are needed. If that be in the lonely farmhouse or the quiet village here on a dull, colorless winter day you are none the less life's heroine."[17]

The voice of tradition espoused by Strauss in her writing was opposed by many women of the day, including those involved in a resurgent national woman's suffrage movement. In 1890 two competing suffrage organizations had united to form the National American Woman Suffrage Association, led by Elizabeth Cady Stanton. Attempting to sway support for its cause, the NAWSA shied away from focusing on women's claims to equal rights as citizens, but argued instead that females should be given the right to vote precisely because of their differences with men. Female morality, the suffragists claimed, would help purify the corrupt world of politics.[18]

Strauss acknowledged that she had received numerous letters— some "quite scolding ones"—from women suffragists criticizing her for her conservative position on the issue of women's rights. As she had in the past, Strauss repeated that she was not an anti-suffragist. "While not wholly convinced of the good of women's having the ballot," she said, "I should not like to stand against any movement that will make the world better or happier." Despite this conciliatory statement, Strauss did disagree with suffragists' claims that giving females the right to vote, finally granted on 26 August 1920 with the Nineteenth Amendment's ratification, would necessarily purify the "muddy pool of politics." Although she regarded her sex highly, noting that a good and bright woman "is a creature a little lower than the angels," Strauss added that not all women are "good, not all honest, not all kind, and their sense of justice is notoriously fallible." Why, she asked, do people suppose that the "franchise would improve women when it certainly does not improve men?" She devoted much of her column detailing some of her reasons for why having the franchise would "cut very little figure in my life" and urging instead the superiority of a simple domestic existence. As one who was afraid of anything that might further disturb what she called "the old-fashioned idea of home," Strauss noted the following:

> Perhaps one reason I have cared so little about suffrage is because I have been so busy making the most of everything that came in my way. Perhaps, too, I care little about it because, personally, I have my liberty. I have it because I took it. Any woman can do the same. She can successfully cultivate a soul liberty that man can scarcely cope with save by like intelligence and understanding. My conception of liberty may not be the proper one and may seem amazing to some women. I am married. We are poor. We probably always will be so, because we are built for it— we lack the quality of making a money success. We have a talent for poverty and can never get away from it, yet I am free, a free moral agent, a free human soul. I can be what I choose to be, think what I choose to think.
>
> I may not be able to govern circumstances, but circumstances shall not govern me. I am an entity, and as such the Universe must recognize me. We do not arrive at this state of liberty by doing things which, at the moment, people call great. We are more likely to find it by sticking to those simple duties that misguided folks call common, and by recognizing limitations we cannot change.[19]

Although she received censure from those advocating women's rights, Strauss became one of the *Journal's* most popular writers. Looking back on her career after her death, the magazine's editors stated that Strauss's influence "was unusually wide" and few writers had ever come so close to its readers as did The Country Contributor. "She was unique," the *Journal* eulogized Strauss, "in her gift of expression."[20] Strauss maintained her rapport with readers by making them feel they were a part of her existence and encouraging them to see the worth of their own lives as homemakers. She managed this feat by revealing through her columns the intimate and mundane details of her family's life in Rockville. An excellent example of Strauss's technique can be found in her piece "A Big Day," which appeared in her book *The Ideas of a Plain Country Woman*. In the essay, she outlined what was, for her, a typical July day that included ironing, cooking, cleaning, baking, feeding the chickens, canning, comforting a hurt child, entertaining a houseguest, assisting a friend at an afternoon reception, comforting a young mother with three crying babies, and putting her own children to bed. Reviewing her "big day," Strauss hoped she could convince people through her example that the "life of the woman who does her own work is not necessarily dull." Dull people, she said, "are born, not made." A country woman, Strauss added, should be thankful for such full days as the one she described and "keep her interest in them just as they are, and she will be to the end immune from the evil days that have no pleasure in them."[21]

Her views on the "manifest destiny" of women as homemakers moderated a bit over the years. Although still persuaded that "wifehood and homekeeping" were "expressive of the thing for which the great majority of women are best fitted," Strauss said she was sure that women would, in the future, go about these duties in quite different ways than those she was used to during her lifetime.[22] She advocated treating household duties as a profession, complete with a salary. "The home—while it may be a place on the door of which is written 'No Admission,' just as it is on the inner sanctuary of a business magnate who needs the quiet and privacy demanded for planning and executing great things—is still a place connected by many live wires with everything that affects the Nation and the race," Strauss said. Her message, however, still included a healthy skepticism toward society and the lure it held to those who lived in the country who read about the doings of literary clubs, dancing clubs, card-playing clubs, and elegant receptions. "What a pity they couldn't initiate their own 'good times,' make their home in the country a place of happy living, glorious thinking, joyous work and the best earthly fulfillment that life affords!" After all, Strauss, too, had been banned from society and ridiculed by club leaders who protested that The Country

Contributor's work in no way reflected the town's culture. "The bar of society . . . could not keep me from having a good time," she noted. "They could not put my eyes out nor stop my ears nor rob me of a personal magnetism that commanded friends. They could not take my work away from me nor hinder me from thinking over the last new book while I hoed out the potatoes and planted corn and beans. They couldn't keep me from having fun with my children and their friends nor from going camping with people I liked, and who, despite my lack of prestige, liked me."[23]

Although Strauss's work may have been mocked by some in her community, it received glowing reviews from the nineteenth state's most popular literary figure in the early twentieth century, the Hoosier Poet, James Whitcomb Riley. The two Indiana writers exchanged numerous letters and invented pet names for each other, with Riley dubbing Strauss "Viola Van Pelt" and himself "Ves Anders." To Riley, Strauss's writing had become so popular with the reading public because of "the simple fact of its being a veritable human document."[24] In addition to praising her work, Riley warned his Rockville friend against overwork. Writing to Strauss on 16 December 1906 Riley offered the following advice:

> but all to myself, near the first glance of the letter, said I,— This happy woman and mother is not so happy as she writes her friends or tells herself with gayest reassurance! *And* I said *this*, too,—She is overworked, and, too proud to even *suspect* it, she even takes on *extra* responsibilities, both mental and physical; and so, said I, if her own doctor don't give her warnin', w'y *I'm* goem to take and turn in and warn her;—and furthermore (lo-and-beholdye!) here is that warnin' now! *Many* a year am I your elder, and know what overwork means, if it's not taken right by the throat and *shuk* loose from quick as the Lord'll let ye![25]

Riley's high regard for Strauss and her writing continued with the publication in 1908 of her book *The Ideas of a Plain Country Woman*. The renowed poet called the work "*just right* everyway." Of course, Riley wrote Strauss, he thought immediately to show the work to her old friend Ves, who responded by proclaiming: "It haint I allers told ye' at that-air Violy was jes the beautiest woman in the world, an' 'at some day the glor'ous tim wuz not fur distant when she'd take an' turn in an' write a whole-indurin' book!"[26] The book also won plaudits from Strauss's rival hometown newspaper, the *Rockville Republican*, which featured an announcement on the book's publication on its front page and noted her "wide reputation as a writer of plain common sense ideas," and from one of her employers, the *Indianapolis News*.[27] A reviewer for the *Indianapolis News* said that the book was filled with words that were good for both men and women to read—"not 'lecturing' words, not discouraging words, but words full of sympathy, help, strength and hope." The reviewer went on to praise Strauss for her "happy, pleasing, intimate style," which made the book a delight to read and "exceedingly entertaining." Strauss herself was commended for bringing the essay form into the average reader's home and the newspaper predicted that the book would "lead many to enjoy this particular class of literature who heretofore have found it somewhat forbidding."[28]

Like Riley's poetry, Strauss's writing found favor with Hoosiers and readers nationwide who moved to urban centers to take advantage of opportunities in business and industry (after 1900 the state's rural population began what one historian called an "abrupt downward slide").[29] True, it was a golden age for literature in Indiana at the turn of the century, but it was also, as John Bartlow Martin notes in his history of the state, a golden age for capitalism. Those who flocked to the cities from the country felt proud about the boom times, but were still nostalgic about their lives in more pastoral settings— settings that Strauss captured so well in her work.[30] Of course, Strauss tempered her homey descriptions of village life with her own hard existence growing up in poverty. Still, her columns in the *Journal* stressed that there were qualities of life existing in country living missing from urban living.

Although she claimed not to be a "misanthrope bewailing the

evils of the times," Strauss nevertheless mourned such changes as the takeover of small businesses by large corporate interests, the swallowing up of the family home by life in apartments and hotels, and the decrease in civility. A day of city life usually was enough to send Strauss "flying home like a bird to its warm nest with a sense of coseyness, of quiet and peace," which she said was the "great essential" of her life.[31] She bewailed the overemphasis in society on material possessions, with young mothers "straining every nerve and fairly driving their husbands mad for the possession of willow plumes and fur coats they can't be happy without," instead of caring for their children.[32] Even with all of its faults, Strauss said she preferred life in her little country village over that of the "tiresome, narrow, sickeningly mediocre ideal of the city and its fatuous knowledge of streetcars and light fixtures and mail-boxes and fire-alarm boxes and jaunty confident manners." She asked why it was that people did not realize that the "plainest countryman, if he is kind and gentle and respectful in his manners to men, women and children, is superior to this cheap standard?"[33]

With her work for Indiana newspapers and a national magazine, Strauss set an exhausting pace for herself, mixing her writing with her responsibilities as a wife and mother. Bessie Skelton, who worked as Strauss's secretary for six years, said that her employer had an "untiring capacity for work" and through the years fell into a regular writing schedule. Strauss set aside Mondays and Tuesdays to produce her columns for the *Indianapolis News* and *Ladies' Home Journal*. "Very seldom did she hesitate about subject matter," Skelton noted. "The words just seemed to flow from the end of her pen. She often said to ambitious and inquiring readers, 'The only way to write is to write:' that was all she could tell them—that was her experience." The middle of the week was a time for dictating replies to letters Strauss received from her readers. Although deluged with correspondence, she made a point to answer every letter. In fact, Strauss had handwritten her replies until the fall of 1912 when she suffered a painful bout of neuritis. "Sometimes her hand would cramp until she could hardly hold the pen," said Skelton. Strauss finally agreed to dictate letters, but Skelton said the writer refused to dictate her columns. "She had formed her habit of thinking and could not change it," she said of Strauss, adding that her employer spent the latter part of the week preparing her "Squibs and Sayings" column for her hometown newspaper.[34] Her work habits were quite different for her other writing activity: poetry. According to her sister Betty, the mood to write verse often came upon Strauss when she felt depressed. "How often I have gone to her house," she noted, "to find her washing the breakfast dishes and at the same time composing verse. She would say she was in the mood for verse, and it nearly always happened that she felt heavy of heart about something."[35]

As she had earlier in her life, Strauss worked doggedly to juggle her writing career and responsibilities as a homemaker. Throughout the week there were constant interruptions in her writing schedule, Skelton noted, including dealing with such details as the dinner menu, where to plant the beets in the garden, and what to have for lunch. "Her two hands were always busy," said the secretary, adding that Strauss seemed to revel in "her domestic life as much as in any other of her numerous lines of work." One thing could and often did interrupt Strauss's regular routine: her children, her grandchildren, and their friends, who often visited the family's home. "Her first and last thought was always for the children—they must have a good, wholesome time—so much would come to them later in life," said Skelton.[36] To Strauss's daughter, Marcia, her mother's writing became so much a part of the family's daily life that "it was merely an accepted thing to us as children, and until I was grown, her unusual ability did not become apparent to me."[37]

Strauss's "passionate love" for her children, according to her daughter Marcia, made them the center of her world. Although she said that her mother tried not to discriminate in this love, there existed between Strauss and her daughter Sarah Katherine "an unusual likeness" in looks as well as in mind, temperament, and even their manner of expression. Sarah Katherine, called Katie and Kate by the family, also had some of her mother's writing talent, winning at age thirteen a medal of honor from *St. Nicholas Magazine* for a poem she contributed to the popular children's periodical. All of this resulted in the formation of a unique tie between the two, said Marcia Strouse. "A telepathic sympathy existed between them at all times," she said of her mother and sister, "and nothing could reconcile either of them to ever so short a separation."[38]

On 28 April 1912, tragedy struck the Strouse family when Sarah Katherine Strouse Henderson, the mother of one son, died at age twenty-five. With Kate's death, said Marcia Strouse, her "mother's existence was completely broken." In writing about Strauss after her death in 1918, Marcia noted that it seemed to her that much of her mother's "physical interest" passed away with Sarah Katherine's death and the "spiritual life, which has been so marked in her work ever since, began and expanded as the spirit which was gone must have developed in brighter surroundings."[39] Her daughter's death struck Strauss so hard that she refused to visit a cabin, called the "Rock River clubhouse," the family had on Sugar Creek. "For it was there [the cabin]," said her sister Betty, "that my sister and her two little girls had many happy summers together—and Gyp just couldn't go back after Kate went away."[40]

Strauss's regular "Squibs and Sayings" column for the weekly *Rockville Tribune* ran alongside her daughter's obituary notice. The column did not mention her daughter's death, but it did stress her continued belief in pushing ahead against all odds. The question is, Strauss reasoned, how to "harmonize yourself with the present moment of existence." The answer lay in doing the "most necessary thing in sight and being glad in the doing of it. By seeing while you are doing it, every bit of beauty in the universe as you know it, and by ignoring the ugliness of your surroundings, and extolling the beauties." Strauss, who believed passionately in the "simple old joys of home and family," took her words to heart in the coming years.[41] It paid off for Strauss and her community as she embarked on a campaign to save from annihilation the natural beauty that Parke County had to offer the state: Turkey Run.

Notes

[1] "Liked Mrs. Strauss's Work," *Indianapolis News*, 28 January 1907.

[2] The Country Contributor, "A Plain Country Woman's Christmas Ideas," *Ladies' Home Journal*, December 1906.

[3] Steinberg, *Reformer in the Marketplace*, 34–36. For more on Bok's life, see "Edward Bok" entry, *Dictionary of American Biography*, vol. 11, supplement 1 (New York: Charles Scribner's Sons, 1944), 91–93; Ernest Schell, "Edward Bok and the *Ladies' Home Journal*," *American History Illustrated* 16 (February 1982):16–23; and David Shi, "Edward Bok and the Simple Life," *American Heritage* 36 (December 1984):100–9.

[4] Edward W. Bok, *A Man from Maine* (New York: Charles Scribner's Sons, 1923), 92.

[5] James Playsted Wood, *The Curtis Magazines* (New York: The Ronald Press Company, 1971), 13. See also, John Tebbel and Mary Ellen Zuckerman, *The Magazine in America, 1741–1990* (New York: Oxford University Press, 1991), 27–38; Kenneth Stewart and John Tebbel, *Makers of Modern Journalism* (New York: Prentice-Hall, Inc., 1952), 199–202; and Helen Damon-Moore, *Magazines for Millions: Gender and Commerce in the* Ladies' Home Journal *and the* Saturday Evening Post, *1880–1910* (Albany, N.Y.: State University of New York Press, 1994), 19–28.

[6] Edward W. Bok, *The Americanization of Edward Bok* (1920, reprint; Philadelphia: Consolidated/Drake Press, 1973), 120–21, 116–17.

[7] Ibid., 117–18. See also, Wood, *The Curtis Magazines*, 21.

[8] Bok, *The Americanization of Edward Bok*, 118.

[9] Shi, "Edward Bok and the Simple Life," 100.

[10] Bok, *The Americanization of Edward Bok*, 124.

[11] Steinberg, *Reformer in the Marketplace*, 55–56.

[12] Louis Filler, *The Muckrakers* (1939, reprint; Stanford, Calif.: Stanford University Press, 1993), 39. See also, Schell, "Edward Bok and the *Ladies' Home Journal*," 22; Shi, "Edward Bok and the Simple Life," 101; and Bok, *The Americanization of Edward Bok*, 246–53.

[13] Steinberg, *Reformer in the Marketplace*, 66–67.

[14] Bok, *The Americanization of Edward Bok*, 219.

[15] Grover Cleveland, "Would Woman Suffrage Be Unwise?" *Ladies' Home Journal*, October 1905. See also, Evans, *Born for Liberty*, 154.

[16] Shi, "Edward Bok and the Simple Life," 101–2. Bok's simple life also entailed a strong reaction against materialism and ostentatious displays of wealth. "There must be," he said, "no imitation of others, no reaching of fancied heights to outdo someone else: no thought of how our mode of living will be judged by others." It may be hard to believe, Bok added, but those who possessed little had the greatest happiness in life over "those who have abundance." Ibid., 102–3.

[17] The Country Contributor, "The Ideas of a Plain Country Woman," *Ladies' Home Journal*, February 1906.

[18] Evans, *Born for Liberty*, 152–54. See also, Glenda Riley, *Inventing the American Woman: An Inclusive History, Volume 2, Since 1877* (Wheeling, Ill.: Harlan Davidson, Inc., 1995), 189–90, and Eleanor Flexner and Ellen Fitzpatrick, *Century of Struggle: The Woman's Rights Movement in the United States* (1959; reprint, Cambridge, Mass.: The Belknap Press of Harvard University Press, 1996), 208–13. The two organizations that merged to form the NAWSA were the National Woman Suffrage Association, originally founded by Stanton and Susan B. Anthony, and the American Woman Suffrage Association, led by Lucy Stone and Julia Ward Howe. The NWSA had advocated pursuing an amendment to the federal constitution to secure women the right to vote, while the AWSA worked for female suffrage through state legislatures. See Evans, *Born for Liberty*, 152.

[19] The Country Contributor, "The Ideas of a Plain Country Woman," *Ladies' Home Journal*, September 1908.

[20] The Country Contributor, "The Ideas of a Plain Country Woman," *Ladies' Home Journal*, December 1918.

[21] Strauss, *The Ideas of a Plain Country Woman*, 188–96.

[22] The Country Contributor, "The Ideas of a Plain Country Woman," *Ladies' Home Journal*, September 1914.

[23] Ibid. See also, "'She is Still Beautiful,' Says Man of Country Contributor," *Indianapolis News*, 10 December 1915.

[24] James Whitcomb Riley to Juliet Strauss, 6 June 1906, Snowden Family Papers, Indiana Historical Society, Indianapolis.

[25] James Whitcomb Riley to Juliet Strauss, 16 December 1906, Snowden Family Papers, IHS. Almost a year later, Riley, via his alter ego Ves Anders, once again warned Strauss about working herself too hard. "'I

see the evidence,'" Riley quoted Ves as saying, "'that she [Strauss] has been, for a long, long time, a-overworking and ort to have a long, long rest—and that's *what!*' he says, a-fetchin' his refined fist down on his dest till he purt-nigh split the *top*!" Riley went on to warn his friend that there was no sense in any gifted writer producing something "jest 'cause they *could* write and the people at made up the what's called *Readin' Public* wanted to keep 'em at it *all* the time—they was no right er reason for 'em just go on a-writin' and a-writin' till they just dropped in their tracks, as the Good Book says." James Whitcomb Riley to Juliet Strauss, 29 November 1907, Snowden Family Papers, IHS.

[26] James Whitcomb Riley to Juliet Strauss, 28 March 1908, Snowden Family Papers, IHS.

[27] "New Book By Juliet V. Strauss," *Rockville Republican*, 25 March 1908.

[28] "'Country Contributor's' Message of Optimism in Book Form," *Indianapolis News*, 28 March 1908.

[29] See Phillips, *Indiana in Transition*, 363.

[30] See, John Bartlow Martin, *Indiana: An Interpretation* (1947; reprint, Bloomington and Indianapolis: Indiana University Press, 1992), 90.

[31] Strauss, *The Ideas of a Plain Country Woman*, 102, 113.

[32] The Country Contributor, "The Ideas of a Plain Country Woman," *Ladies' Home Journal*, September 1912.

[33] The Country Contributor, "The Ideas of a Plain Country Woman," *Ladies' Home Journal*, April 1908.

[34] Bessie Skelton, "Mrs. Strauss at Work," *Rockville Tribune Memorial Supplement*, 4 June 1918.

[35] William Herschell, "State Park Head Urges Memorial to Juliet V. Strauss at Turkey Run," *Indianapolis News*, 1 June 1918.

[36] Skelton, "Mrs. Strauss at Work," *Rockville Tribune Memorial Supplement*, 4 June 1918.

[37] Ott, "Some Memories of My Mother," *Rockville Tribune Memorial Supplement*, 4 June 1918.

[38] Ibid.

[39] Ibid. See also, "Kate Strouse Henderson," *Rockville Tribune*, 30 April 1912.

[40] Herschell, "State Park Head Urges Memorial," *Indianapolis News*, 1 June 1918.

[41] Juliet V. Strauss, "Squibs and Sayings," *Rockville Tribune*, 30 April 1912.

John Lusk at his Turkey Run property

John Lusk looks warily at the camera

Juliet Strauss (atop horse) portrays an early settler at the Parke County pageant celebrating the nineteenth state's centennial

The first Christian marriage in Parke County—part of the county's pageant to commemorate Indiana's statehood centennial

Turkey Run Hollow

A group enjoys Sugar Creek at Turkey Run, 5 August 1914

Indiana State Library

Richard Lieber at Turkey Run

Juliet Strauss later in life

The Woman's Press Club of Indiana unveils the *Subjugation* statue in
memory of Juliet Strauss at Turkey Run State Park, 2 July 1922

IN MEMORIAM
JULIET V. STRAUSS - "THE COUNTRY CONTRIBUTOR"
BY
THE WOMAN'S PRESS CLUB OF INDIANA

The *Subjugation* statue, designed by Myra Richards

Chapter Five
TURKEY RUN

In the spring of 1826, Captain Salmon Lusk, a soldier who served under General William Henry Harrison at the Battle of Tippecanoe, traveled north from Fort Harrison in Vigo County with his wife in search of land on which to make their home. The couple settled near Sugar Creek in what is now Parke County, a stream the Native Americans had called Pungosecone, "the waters of many sugar trees." For his service in the War of 1812, Lusk was given approximately 1,400 acres by the federal government. Alongside the creek on a spot known as the "Narrows," Lusk built a mill to grind flour, which was loaded on flatboats and taken to be sold in New Orleans and other southern cities. Lusk, who also dabbled in the pork-packing business, prospered enough to build a fine brick home for his family, which included his son John, on a hill overlooking Sugar Creek. The area encompassing the Lusk homestead became known to Parke County residents as Turkey Run for the thousands of wild turkeys that gathered to seek protection under the overhanging rocks that dotted the landscape.[1]

Upon Salmon Lusk's death, a large part of the land known as Turkey Run—which included magnificent stands of beech, walnut, sycamore, maple, poplar, and oak trees—became the property of the old captain's only living son, John (another son, Salmon Jr., had been killed during the Civil War as a member of the Eighty-Fifth Indiana Regiment). Educated as a young man at the Waveland Academy, Lusk as a young man traveled west for a time to work in the gold mines, returning home, according to one account, with a large amount of the precious metal. Described as a "very peculiar and eccentric man" who permitted no hunting or trapping on his land, Lusk neverthe-less welcomed visitors to enjoy the natural charms that abounded on his property. Resisting offers for his land from various timber compa-nies, Lusk did allow a railroad company, the Indianapolis, Decatur & Springfield Railroad, to lease a portion of his land for a summer resort. In 1881 and 1882, the railroad constructed an eating house and set up tents for the guests who flocked to the resort advertised as "Bloomingdale Glens," the name by which the area came to be known by outsiders (Parke County residents still called the land Turkey Run). For financial reasons, the railroad eventually gave up its lease and Lusk leased the resort to his friend William Hooghkirk, who ran the vacation spot from 1884 until 1910. With his health failing, Hooghkirk turned over the resort's management to R. P. Luke in 1910.[2]

The Turkey Run area became a favorite gathering place for Parke County residents, particularly during holidays like the Fourth of July. One of the largest events held there was a two-day Civil War reunion in 1880, which included a sham battle fought between the Union veterans and the McCune cadets.[3] Enoch P. Shrigley, born and raised in Rockville, recalled that rich and poor people alike from all over the state flocked to witness Turkey Run's beauty in the early 1910s. Those with means from Terre Haute drove "gleaming Packards, Wintons, Pierce-Arrows, Locomobiles and other prestigious vehicles" and dressed in linen dusters and wore goggles as they sped through Rockville on their way to commune with nature. They "glanced dis-dainfully, if at all," said Shrigley, "at the gaping peasants who paused to marvel at their magnificence." Those less affluent folks had to content themselves with Model T Fords and horse-drawn wagons and buggies as means of transportation to the site, he added. Shrigley particularly remembered one visit to Turkey Run he made for a pic-nic with his Sunday school class as a boy. The ride to the area, re-markable in itself for the vistas it afforded the youngster, "paled into insignificance," he said, when his party reached Turkey Run. He noted:

Those trees, those giant trees, standing thickly about! Their huge trunks, some of them soaring upward for a hundred feet or more, were like the columns of a vast cathedral. Their leafy crowns, merging far above in a riot of leaves and boughs, were like its ceiling. The soft breezes of summer, sighing gently through the tree-tops, were like the whisper of angels' wings and seemed to accentuate, rather than disturb, the holy quiet. Even the myriad colorful birds, flitting happily about, seemed to sing with muted voices as if loathe to break the awesome silence. Surely, if God had walked again upon the earth, he would have chosen to wander here amongst these cool and shady forest aisles.[4]

The cathedral of trees described by Shrigley was in grave peril in March 1915 with John Lusk's death. For several years before Lusk's demise, people in the Rockville community had urged Lusk to consider giving his beautiful landholdings to the state for use as a park or forest preserve. In March 1914 Howard Maxwell, a Rockville lawyer, wrote former vice president Charles W. Fairbanks, then out of political office but one of the founders of the Indiana Forestry Association and the group's president. In his letter, Maxwell asked Fairbanks if he might contact Lusk, either via letter or in person, and convince him to, upon his death, leave his property to the state and not to his relatives. "The citizens of this place and of the County generally are concerned about the matter," said Maxwell, "because they know that it is only a matter of a few years until the ownership will go out of Mr. Lusk's hands and if it falls into the hands of his kindred it means that these magnificent trees will be sold for commercial purpose, for the high dollar." Lusk, noted Maxwell, was a "great admirer" of Fairbanks, but he went on to warn the Hoosier Republican that the taboo subjects he should avoid in talking with the "eccentric old bachelor" included women, secret societies (especially Masons), corruption in politics, and extravagance in government.[5]

Although Fairbanks responded favorably to Maxwell's request, noting it would be "a great pity to have it [Turkey Run] sacrificed to gratify commercial greed," Lusk died before any agreement could be reached on turning his land over to the state.[6] And, with R. P. Luke's lease on the land set to expire in 1917, it looked as if Turkey Run's splendor might fall into the hands of the timber interests. It was then that another Rockville native—Strauss—took matters into her own hands. Strauss had held a special place in her heart for Turkey Run ever since her days as a young girl tromping through the wooded wonderland. "What a place for childhood those cool canyons have always been," she said. "How the children of generations past have played and waded there, for the water in the glens is not deep enough for danger at any place. Its stepping stones offering glad opportunities for holding hands in all seasons." In fact, Strauss added, any girl who lived near Turkey Run and had not been proposed to there at least once "has been a very poor manager since the place itself suggests lovemaking as it suggests rest, fulfillment and such explanation of God's purposes that we always find in lovely spots where simple eyesight and hearing and breathing seem a good enough reason for having lived."[7]

On 15 April 1915 Indiana governor Samuel M. Ralston, a member of the Democratic party, received from Strauss "an inspiring letter describing eloquently and graphically the beauties of Turkey Run and closing her communication with a passionate appeal for me as Governor to take steps to have preserved for future generations this historic place."[8] Ralston, who considered Strauss "one of Indiana's most gifted women," had also received a similar request from the Indiana Federation of Clubs' conservation department; he lost no time in acting on the pleas for help. On 27 April 1915 the governor appointed Strauss, William W. Woollen of Indianapolis, and Vida Newsom of Columbus to a Turkey Run Commission and charged them with the task of examining the Bloomingdale Glens area and report back to him on what "can be done by themselves or the State or both to preserve the natural beauty of this place and keep it as a habitation of the wild life of the woods, and as a restful retreat for man: to the end that here the young may find romance, older folks rest and all recreation and a renewing of the spirit, through a real communion with nature."[9]

In spite of its auspicious beginnings, the commission, which had no legislative authority, floundered. Fortunately for the commission and Turkey Run, Ralston had not been the only person to whom Strauss had pleaded for aid in saving Parke County's natural wonder. The Rockville writer had also expressed her concerns to her colleagues at the *Indianapolis News*, who included editor Richard Smith. Smith turned for help to an Indianapolis man who had written an editorial for the newspaper in 1910 protesting the destruction of trees cut down to widen a thoroughfare: Richard Lieber. Smith asked to see Lieber and the following conversation ensued:

> "Juliet Strauss . . . has been weeping on my shoulder. She says Turkey Run is going to be cut up. Have you seen those trees?"
>
> "Where is Turkey Run?" Richard [Lieber] asked.
>
> "Darned if I know," answered Mr. Smith, "but Juliet knows all about it."
>
> "You don't mean Bloomingdale Glens?" Richard asked.
>
> "Yes, that's it. That's what we've got to save."[10]

In enlisting the German-born Lieber's help, Smith had recruited a person who became an indispensable ally in the battle for Turkey Run and the leading force in the development of Indiana's state park system. Born in Saint Johann-Saarbrueckn, Germany, on 5 September 1869, Lieber came to America in 1891. Upon settling in Indianapolis, where his uncles Herman and Albert Lieber operated the Indianapolis Brewing Company, Richard Lieber first found work as a clerk for Franke and Schindler's hardware store. Later, he helped found the Western Chemical Company, served as the music and art critic for the *Indianapolis Journal*, and started his own bottling and soft drink company. His interest in preserving the nation's natural resources was fueled in part by trips he took out west to California,

Idaho, and Montana. Closer to home, in September 1910, while visiting a cabin in Brown County owned by his friend Fred Hetherington, Lieber had been so impressed by the area's scenic wonders that he boldly stated the "whole county ought to be bought up by the State and then made into a State Park so that all of the people of Indiana could enjoy this beauty spot." He recalled that it was in Brown County that he had "heard the call to bestir myself and build our Indiana State Parks." Later, he bought his own cabin in Brown County (named Whip poor will Lodge) and, in October 1912, was chairman for the local board of governors for the Fourth National Conservation Congress, held that year in Indianapolis.[11]

After his talk with Smith, Lieber set out to meet with the man who controlled the Turkey Run Commission: Ralston. In November 1915 he talked with the governor and laid out his vision for a state park system. To Lieber, a statewide park system would "not only memorialize the past but would build for the future by practical conservation. They [parks] would distinctly point out the desirability of preserving trees, of protecting birds and animal life." By opening these natural areas to the general public, he added, Hoosiers would realize that "wastefulness of Nature's beauties and treasures is out of harmony with the spirit of the time, progress and the needs of Indiana's new century." As examples for his state park idea, Lieber pointed to successful ventures in Massachusetts, Maine, New York, California, and Wisconsin. "In all of these States, as it would be in Indiana," he said, "the chief purpose of State Parks is to refresh and strengthen and renew tired people, and fit them for the common round of daily life." State parks also held another benefit, Lieber said—money. He noted that there "is a cash value in scenery," as income could be derived from park visitors, from special concessions, and from sales of fish and game permits. In turn, this income, Lieber argued, could then be used to help fund park maintenance.[12]

Lieber's dreams for Indiana state parks won fast approval from Ralston, perhaps because the budding conservationist allied his parks plan with a project near and dear to the governor's heart: the commemoration of Indiana's statehood centennial. A state park system, Lieber reasoned, would serve as a permanent memorial to the centennial celebration.[13] As a newspaper reporter, Lieber also knew the value of good press and used it to his advantage with the park plan. Lieber shared his idea for a statewide park system with Enos Mills, a Colorado naturalist who had lived in Indianapolis as a boy and had worked to create Rocky Mountain National Park. While he was in Washington, D.C., on a visit, Mills, in a story that appeared in the *Indianapolis News* on 17 November 1915, called for the creation of three state parks in Indiana—Brown County, Turkey Run, and the dunes area in the northwest portion of the state—as a fitting part of the state centennial celebration. To celebrate the anniversary without taking "definite steps to make permanent state reservations of the primeval wildness that still exists in three places in the state would," Mills stated, "be no celebration at all, in my opinion." In recalling the Mills article, Lieber said that he had the "sneaking suspicion that he [Mills] just said the first paragraph or two, and that Richard Smith and myself added all the rest."[14] It worked. Ralston appointed Lieber and businessman Albert Cannon of Marshall, Indiana, to the Turkey Run Commission on 14 January 1916.

The appointments were heartily approved by Strauss, who had written the governor just five days before the new men joined the commission to complain that "since Mr. Woollen does not seem to go after the thing as he might and Miss Newsom does nothing at all, and I am sort of a flash in the pan myself in the little I have tried to do, that it might be a good thing to appoint two more people on the Commission." She added that at first she had thought about resigning from the group in favor of "somebody who could be more active in the Commission, but so many people declare that I must not resign. I want to be of service if I can."[15]

In acquiescing to Lieber's state park plans, Ralston might have been attempting to bolster the centennial celebration, something he had been a leading force in for some time. When Hoosier voters in November 1914 voted overwhelmingly (466,700 to 97,718) against appropriating two million dollars to commemorate the statehood centennial by constructing a memorial building to house the State Library and other historical agencies, Ralston argued that the memorial plan had been defeated not because Indiana's citizens were against celebrating the state's one hundredth birthday, but because they objected "to the amount of money sought to be appropriated therefor."[16] At Ralston's request, the Indiana General Assembly in 1915 agreed to appropriate $25,000 and create a nine-member Indiana Historical Commission to promote the centennial celebration. The legislature's financial support for the commission marked the first time the state had committed significant funds to history. Of the $25,000 supplied by the state, $20,000 was earmarked for the promotion of centennial activities, with the remaining $5,000 (called a "beggarly amount" by Indiana historian Dunn) for collecting, editing, and publishing Indiana's history.[17]

The IHC worked hard to make the centennial celebration a success, blitzing the state with a wide array of publicity and educational efforts. Special bulletins were sent to county school superintendents asking for their cooperation; direct appeals were made to teachers in the summer and fall of 1915; a weekly IHC newsletter began publication; and commission members addressed various clubs, civic organizations, churches, and historical societies (commission member Charity Dye of Indianapolis alone gave 152 talks). Along with sponsoring a film on the state, titled "Indiana," which featured beloved poet Riley telling the story of the state's development to a group of children, the IHC used the services of a number of other Hoosier authors—George Ade, Meredith Nicholson, Booth Tarkington, Gene Stratton-Porter, and others—to issue a call for former Indiana residents to return to the state for the centennial celebration.

With a successful publicity campaign under way, the commission next turned its attention to how to best stage the actual celebration, keeping in mind that with the scarcity of funds available such events would have to be financed by individual communities. The commission soon found an answer: historical pageants. These live dramas appealed strongly to the IHC as a way to focus attention on Indiana's history and provide a way to bring communities together. The commission hired William Chauncy Langdon, former first president of the American Pageant Association, as the State Pageant Master. Langdon, who considered the pageant as "a distinct and individual art form, having its own laws and its own technique," wrote and directed three pageants—at Indiana University, held 16–18 May 1916; at the old state capital of Corydon, performed 2–3 June 1916; and one in Indianapolis, presented 2–7 October 1916.[18] With aid from the IHC, counties around the state also held their own pageants, with forty-five county or local pageants presented in 1916 seen by an estimated 250,000 people.[19] Strauss noted that when Parke County planned its pageant, everybody wanted to perform (she portrayed an early settler on horseback). Discussing the county's enthusiasm for the project with her daughter one day, Strauss recalled that her granddaughter, slated to play the part of a Native American "papoosie," gravely asked: "Mother, who is going to watch?"[20]

The commission's crowning achievement, however, came when it latched on to Lieber's idea of creating state parks as a way to give the centennial celebration a lasting contribution. At its January 1916 meeting, the IHC approved a formal motion in favor of inaugurating a movement for state parks and, two months later, selected Lieber as head of a park committee (the group absorbed the Turkey Run Commission). In accepting Lieber's vision, the IHC reasoned that state parks would not only be a "splendid present day expression of appreciation of what the Hoosier forefathers wrought," but also that they would have "a high civic value" in the present and the future by "strengthening . . . the common bonds of citizenship and neighborly association, for in these parks the people will meet upon common ground."[21]

The park committee's first meeting on 19 March 1916 saw the group spring into "immediate action," Lieber noted, because Lusk's heirs were to auction off the Turkey Run area in just sixty days. Time was of the essence due to the interest of various timber companies who were after ten or twelve large black walnut trees at Turkey Run valued at approximately $15,000. The firms were supposedly planning to use wood from the trees for gunstocks, then in demand for use in World War I.[22] With no money forthcoming from the legislature, the committee had to raise funds to purchase the Parke County land from the public. To secure the land, the park committee and the IHC set as a goal the raising of $25,000. As he had done in promoting the idea for a state park system, Lieber skillfully used newspapers throughout Indiana to publicize the committee's efforts. Ralston lent a hand by proclaiming the week beginning 24 April 1916 as the time for the state's citizens to make contributions to the State Park Fund, and the committee received endorsements from such respected figures as President Woodrow Wilson, Vice President Thomas Marshall (a Strauss friend), former President Theodore Roosevelt, United States senators Thomas Taggart and John W. Kern (another Strauss confidant), *Atlantic Monthly* editor Ellery Sedgwick, and a host of illustrious Indiana writers and congressmen.[23]

Close to the date for the Turkey Run auction, however, Lieber and his committee had fallen short of their goal, receiving approximately $20,000 in donations. "I am pained to acknowledge," Lieber reported, "that the citizens of the State generally did not respond in a manner which can possibly be compared to the liberality of the citizens of Indianapolis."[24] Parke County residents, however, did open their pocketbooks to save Turkey Run, contributing a total of $2,000. Even with the shortfall in funds, Lieber, who had personally given $1,000, remained optimistic that the committee would be able to save Turkey Run.[25] He wrote Strauss in April 1916 that the committee knew financially it would be in a position to bid on Turkey Run "if opposing bidders do not run the price up to an extravagant point. We think that Indiana bidders are going to see the civic side and help rather than hinder us, but we do not know what to expect in the way of opposition from timber men from outside the State. We may not have any opposition from them. So unless unforeseen circumstances arise, we are satisfied we will get Turkey Run."[26]

Those "unforeseen circumstances" cropped up on the day of the bidding for Turkey Run on 18 May 1916. Under clear, sunny skies, more than two thousand people were on hand for the auction, which was held on the porch of the old Lusk homestead. "The day was ideal—many auto loads went through Rockville that day to the auction, and many others came there by different routes," the *Rockville Tribune* reported. "Most of the people who could get away that day went up from Rockville to see what they thought was going to be a memorable occasion in State history." Even some cameramen were on the scene to record the event for the state centennial film, the newspaper added.[27] Richard Lieber's wife, Emma, could not "remember a more exciting day in all my life; I finally became so enthusiastic that I was eager to give up any piece of jewelry, in fact, anything I possessed just to help outbid those agents who were bidding against the park committee."[28]

The auction started at one o'clock in the afternoon with the Lusk property divided into seven tracts, with Tract Number Three, the Turkey Run land totaling 288 acres, as the main prize for bidders and reserved as the last item up for bid. With most of the other tracts successfully obtained by the Hoosier Veneer Company of Indianapolis for $37,500, most of the other timber companies at the auction from Indiana and Illinois refrained from bidding when the Turkey Run tract came up for bid. The Hoosier Veneer Company, along with the Lusk heirs and the Park Committee, represented by its secretary and Indianapolis attorney Leo M. Rappaport (Lieber's brother-in-law), fought against one another to win the land. Herschell, who covered the auction for the *Indianapolis News*, described the bidding:

> The [Lusk] heirs held the top bid at $30,000. Shorty Burks [the auctioneer] kept calling for more money, asking for $100 a bid.
>
> "Thirty thousand dollars! Make it thirty thousand one hundred!" Shorty pleaded.
>
> There was a silence—a seemingly interminable silence.

"One hundred dollars more Leo," Mr. Lieber said under his breath. "One hundred dollars more and then—quit."

That word "quit" sounded like the tolling of a bell for a well beloved friend. Mr. Rappaport made the bid $30,100. The Hoosier Veneer Company's man, as quick as a flash, added the fatal $100, running the price up to $30,200. This seemed like a slap in the face to the state park committee, for only yesterday the Hoosier Veneer Company, through Harry Daugherty, the president, gave $100 to the state park committee to be used at Turkey Run. And now another $100 of Hoosier Veneer money had swept away the hopes of the people.

"Turkey Run is dead," said Mr. Lieber. "Long live the state park movement."[29]

The fight to save Turkey Run, however, was far from over. The fighting spirit that Herschell observed in Strauss when he came upon her with her tear-stained face after the auction, was shared by the park committee, especially Lieber, and the governor. Upon returning to Indianapolis, Lieber met with those committee members who lived in the city and told them, prophetically it turned out, that although they had lost Turkey Run that day, it did not mean "that we have given up hope of persuading the lumber company to see the light. Some day we will own Turkey Run."[30] Ralston shared Lieber's optimism and fierce determination to secure the land for the state. Responding to a letter from Strauss in which she had indicated that he could be the most popular governor Indiana ever had if he could "cinch Turkey Run," Ralston told her that he was "desperately in earnest to have the honor you suggest, and there is nothing short of committing a crime that I will not do to secure this honor and incidentally this park." One way or the other, Ralston added, the state "will ultimately come into possession of this beauty spot."[31]

The park committee did have some time on their side, as R. P. Luke held a lease on the Turkey Run property until April 1917 and the veneer company could not take possession until after that date. Just a few days after the auction, the committee learned of two encouraging developments. First, Carl Fisher, one of the Indianapolis Motor Speedway owners, wrote Lieber pledging to give the state park memorial fund 10 percent of the net profits from the sixth annual Indianapolis 500, provided that the Turkey Run property "is released to your committee in its present condition at the actual cost price by the corporation which purchased it on the 18th inst." Also, Daugherty wrote Governor Ralston and made a three-part proposal that included possible future action by the legislature to reimburse the company for the property, a plan whereby the veneer firm would remove the saw timber from the tract and then deed the property free of cost to the state, and an offer whereby the company could remove one hundred "choice trees" from the tract and "then deed the property free of cost to the state park board."[32]

In making his proposal to the park committee, Daugherty defended his company's actions, noting that the "fact that we bought a flourishing woodland is not to be construed as an indication that we have no interest in the preservation of beautiful park sites either because of their scenic value or because they may be made into a forest reservation. In fact, our business is such that we must approve any movement looking to the conservation of forests."[33] Although the committee rejected the Hoosier Veneer Company's proposal, negotiations on the property continued. In spite of Daugherty's conciliatory words, the company's actions had rubbed some Hoosiers the wrong way, including Strauss, who wrote Ralston and asked if anything could be done to make Daugherty "see what a burning disgrace to Indiana here in our Centennial year this affair is? Now you can't imagine the feeling that exists throughout the state towards the Hoosier Veneer Co. I believe people would lynch Daugherty if they had a leader."[34]

While negotiations continued on the Turkey Run property, the committee had the opportunity to purchase the rugged area of McCormick's Creek in Owen County, known as "Indiana's Grand Canyon" for the mile-long, one-hundred-foot-deep canyon that ran through the area. First settled by the McCormick family, who registered the land in 1816, the scenic area later became home to a resort and sanitarium operated by Dr. Fredrick William Denkewalter (the modern-day Canyon Inn now stands on the site of the sanitarium). A graduate of Rush Medical College, Denkewalter had practiced medicine and had run a drugstore in Indianapolis before moving to Owen County in 1888, constructing his sanitarium that same year. With Denkewalter's death, as in the case of Turkey Run, the land was to be auctioned off to the highest bidder.[35]

The committee acted at once to secure the Owen County property, but this time the group was wiser from its Turkey Run experience. Learning that the land's appraised price was $5,250, and after visiting the site, the committee decided to buy McCormick's Creek "provided that the citizens of Owen County," noted Lieber, "would raise one-fourth of the purchase price among themselves and would guarantee that the cost would not exceed the appraisement."[36] The county's residents were successful in their fund-raising efforts and the committee sent Rappaport to Spencer to bid on the property. Not wishing a repeat of the heartbreak he suffered at Turkey Run, Rappaport sought out the son of the deceased owner and warned him that "so far as I was concerned, I would not bid more than the appraised value. He argued with me at some length and told me that for face saving purposes, he had to enter the bidding, and I finally agreed with him that I had no objections to this, provided he fully understood that if he bid even one dollar more than the appraised value, he, and not our group, would be the purchaser." The next morning the first bid for the land was for $5,000, followed by successive raises by the Denkewalter heir and Rappaport of $50 until the parks committee representative made the final winning bid of $5,250. McCormick's Creek became Indiana's first state park and, as Rappaport noted, the "son of the decedent and I parted as friends."[37]

As negotiations with the timber company dragged on, the committee discovered that soliciting donations from Hoosiers was becoming harder and harder. Some people who had originally donated money to help buy Turkey Run even wrote Lieber demanding a refund. The money problems saddened Lieber and angered Strauss, who wrote him that people were "not awake to the importance of the [park] movement. The American spirit of personal selfishness and greed for the dollar have so permeated our people that it is difficult to get them to look at the thing in the right light."[38] The committee, however, did receive, as promised, substantial financial support from the Indianapolis Motor Speedway Association, which donated $5,065, along with an additional $5,000 from Arthur Newby, one of the Speedway's founders. On 11 November 1916 the committee finally reached a settlement with the Hoosier Veneer Company, purchasing Turkey Run for $40,200, giving the Indianapolis company a $10,000 profit. Rappaport, who worked with Lieber and Sol Kiser and Frank B. Wynn, committee members, to secure the purchase, said that the agreement reached was a fair one. "I am convinced . . . that the timber values on the Turkey Run tract alone are worth all that we have paid," said Rappaport. "Adding to this the value which is derived from the fact that this timber could not be replaced if it were once cut down, and that we have preserved for the coming generations of our state a product of nature such as Turkey Run is. I feel that we have obtained a bargain at the price which we have paid."[39] The final piece came in 1917 when the state legislature appropriated $20,000 to use in conjunction with the purchase of Turkey Run, McCormick's Creek, and any other state park that might be created. Indiana finally had a state park system.[40]

With Turkey Run saved, Lieber turned his attention to winning approval from the General Assembly for his comprehensive plan for an Indiana Department of Conservation, which would be responsible for the state park system and include geology, entomology, forestry, lands and waters, and fish and game divisions. The plan met with rejection by the 1917 legislature but won approval two years later, and Lieber became head of the new department.[41] But Strauss, whose "sturdiness of soul was one of the strong factors in the fight" for Turkey Run and who considered the area her "religion," as her friend Herschell noted, would not be around to witness Lieber's conservation victory.[42] Her struggles to save the land she loved would, however, win for her in the coming years a measure of immortality.

Notes

[1] For a history of Turkey Run, the Lusk family, and efforts to preserve the area, see, The Department of Conservation, *Turkey Run State Park*, 8–11, 36–39; "John Lusk Dead. One of Parke County's Largest Land Holders, Owner of Turkey Run and an Eccentric Character Dies at His Home in Sugar Creek Township," *Rockville Tribune*, 23 March 1915; Robert Allen Frederick, "Colonel Richard Lieber, Conservationist and Park Builder: The Indiana Years" (Ph.D. diss., Indiana University, 1960), 113; Suellen M. Hoy, "Governor Samuel M. Ralston and Indiana's Centennial Celebration," *Indiana Magazine of History* 71 (September 1975):253–54; Hoy, "Samuel M. Ralston: Progressive Governor, 1913–1917," (Ph.D. diss., Indiana University, 1975), 199–200; and Boomhower, "Celebrating Statehood: The Indiana Centennial of 1916," *Traces of Indiana and Midwestern History* 3 (summer, 1991):38–39.

[2] See, "John Lusk Dead," *Rockville Tribune*, 23 March 1915, and Department of Conservation, *Turkey Run State Park*, 10–11. In detailing Lusk's life, the *Rockville Tribune* gave as an example of the man's eccentric character his belief that members of "secret societies" had the power to "throw out poison—that he [Lusk] used oil taken from a furbearing animal to counteract the venom and that on a number of occasions had jumped into the waters of Sugar Creek when meeting a man wearing the Masonic charm." The newspaper did acknowledge that if a person ever did Lusk a favor he never forgot the kindness and that he possessed a strong constitution. Lusk often would ride on horseback the four miles from his home to Marshall, put the animal in a livery stable, and walk seven miles to Rockville to purchase supplies. He would remain in Rockville, according to the *Rockville Tribune*'s account, until late at night "when he would start afoot, with probably a hundred pounds on his shoulders, to Marshall, where he mounted his horse and rode home." See, "John Lusk Dead," *Rockville Tribune*, 23 March 1915.

[3] Strouse, "Turkey Run," in *Parke County Centennial Memorial*, 96.

[4] Enoch P. Shrigley, "Forum: The Readers Corner," *Indianapolis Star Magazine*, 19 August 1973.

[5] Howard Maxwell to Charles W. Fairbanks, 12 March 1914, Indiana Forestry Association Papers, Lilly Library, Indiana University, Bloomington.

[6] Charles W. Fairbanks to Howard Maxwell, 18 March 1914, Indiana Forestry Association Papers, Lilly Library, Indiana University, Bloomington.

[7] See William Leo Lieber, "Colonel Richard Lieber and Turkey Run State Park," Lecture at Indiana Historical Society's 21st Annual Indiana History Workshop, 1971, Turkey Run State Park, 8.

[8] See, Frederick, "Colonel Richard Lieber," 114–15; Hoy, "Governor Samuel M. Ralston and Indiana's Centennial Celebration," 253; and "State Parks Win Ralston's Praise," *Indianapolis News*, 9 August 1924.

[9] Turkey Run Commission, 27 April 1915, Samuel Ralston Papers, Indiana State Archives, Commission on Public Records, Indianapolis. See also, "Preserve Turkey Run," *Rockville Tribune*, 4 May 1915, and "Would Preserve Old Beauty Spot," *Indianapolis Star*, 28 April 1915.

[10] Emma Lieber, *Richard Lieber* (Indianapolis: n.p., 1947), 80. See also, Frederick, "Colonel Richard Lieber," 115–16; Hoy, "Samuel M. Ralston: Progressive Governor," 200; and "Struggles of Founding State Park System are Recalled," *Indianapolis News*, 1 December 1941.

[11] See, Richard Lieber, *America's Natural Wealth: A Story of the Use and Abuse of Our Resources* (New York: Harper & Brothers Publishers, 1942), xiv; William Lieber, "Colonel Richard Lieber and Turkey Run State Park," 2–3, Hoy, "Samuel M. Ralston: Progressive Governor," 200–1; Frederick, "Colonel Richard Lieber," 9–15; Giles Hoyt, "Richard Lieber," *Encyclopedia of Indianapolis*, 907–8; Dunn, *Indiana and Indianans*, 5:2219–21; and David M. Silver, ed., "Richard Lieber and Indiana's Forest Heritage," *Indiana Magazine of History* 67 (March 1971):45–55.

[12] Richard Lieber, "Report of Park Committee of the Indiana Historical Commission," in Lindley, ed., *The Indiana Centennial*, 53–55.

[13] See, Hoy, "Samuel M. Ralston: Progressive Governor," 201, and Frederick, "Colonel Richard Lieber," 116.

[14] See, "Struggles of Founding State Park System Are Recalled," *Indianapolis News*, 1 December 1941; "Creation of State Parks Advocated," *Indianapolis News*, 17 November 1915; and Frederick, "Colonel Richard

Lieber," 116–17.

[15] Juliet V. Strauss to Samuel M. Ralston, 9 January 1916, Ralston Papers, Indiana State Archives, Commission on Public Records.

[16] Hoy, "Governor Samuel Ralston and Indiana's Centennial Celebration," 246.

[17] See, Lana Ruegamer, *A History of the Indiana Historical Society, 1830–1980* (Indianapolis: Indiana Historical Society, 1980), 103, and Dunn, *Indiana and Indianans* 2:781. Joining Ralston on the nonsalaried IHC were Frank B. Wynn, former chairman of a 1911 centennial committee; Harlow Lindley, director of the department of Indiana History and Archives of the Indiana State Library; James A. Woodburn, director of the Indiana Historical Survey of Indiana University; the Reverend John Cavanaugh, president of the University of Notre Dame; Charles W. Moores, first vice president of the Indiana Historical Society; Samuel Foster, Fort Wayne; Lew O'Bannon, Corydon (grandfather of Indiana Governor Frank O'Bannon); and Charity Dye, an Indianapolis schoolteacher. The commission also employed Professor Walter C. Woodward, Earlham College, to direct the centennial celebration and Lucy M. Elliott as assistant director. See, Lindley, *The Indiana Centennial*, and, Boomhower, "Celebrating Statehood," 32–33.

[18] William Chauncy Langdon, *The Pageant of Indiana: The Development of the State as a Community from its Exploration by LaSalle to the Centennial of its Admission to the Union* (Indianapolis: The Hollenbeck Press, 1916), Foreword.

[19] Lindley, *The Indiana Centennial*, 40.

[20] The Country Contributor, "The Ideas of a Plain Country Woman," *Ladies' Home Journal*, August 1916.

[21] Lindley, *The Indiana Centennial*, 47.

[22] See, "Bidders for Turkey Run at Scenic Wonderland," *Indianapolis News*, 18 May 1916.

[23] See, Richard Lieber, "Report of Park Committee," *The Indiana Centennial*, 50; Frederick, "Colonel Richard Lieber," 120–21; Hoy, "Governor Samuel Ralston and Indiana's Centennial Celebration," 256; and Hoy, "Samuel M. Ralston: Progressive Governor," 202–3.

[24] Richard Lieber, "Report of Park Committee," *The Indiana Centennial*, 50.

[25] See, Strouse, *Parke County Centennial Memorial*, 96.

[26] Frederick, "Colonel Richard Lieber," 125.

[27] "Turkey Run Lost. Hoosier Veneer Company Buys Parke County's Famous Summer Resort for $30,200," *Rockville Tribune*, 23 May 1916. See also, Hoy, "Governor Samuel M. Ralston: Progressive Governor," 257.

[28] Emma Lieber, *Richard Lieber*, 86.

[29] "Turkey Run Sold to Timber Man," *Indianapolis News*, 19 May 1916. See also, "Tract Sold to Makers of Veneer," *Indianapolis Star*, 19 May 1916. The *Indianapolis Star* reported in its article on the auction that the Hoosier Veneer Company planned to use eight large walnut trees located in the Turkey Run tract not for gunstocks for the European conflict, but for veneer for piano cases. Ibid.

[30] Emma Lieber, *Richard Lieber*, 87.

[31] Samuel M. Ralston to Juliet V. Strauss, 31 May 1916, Samuel M. Ralston Papers, Lilly Library, Indiana University, Bloomington.

[32] "Important Moves in Parks Project," *Indianapolis News*, 23 May 1916. See also, Frederick, "Colonel Richard Lieber," 131.

[33] "State May Save Turkey Run Site," *Indianapolis Star*, 24 May 1916.

[34] Juliet V. Strauss to Samuel Ralston, 27 May 1916, Ralston Papers, Lilly Library, Indiana University, Indianapolis. See also, Hoy, "Governor Samuel Ralston: Progressive Governor," 258.

[35] See, *Owen County, Indiana: A History* (Spencer, Ind.: Owen County Historical and Genealogical Society, 1994), 18, and Department of Conservation, State of Indiana, *McCormick's Creek Canyon State Park: A History and Description* (Indianapolis: William B. Burford, Contractor of State Printing and Binding, 1923), 6–9.

[36] Richard Lieber, "Report of Park Committee," *The Indiana Centennial*, 53.

[37] Frederick, "Colonel Richard Lieber," 130.

[38] Ibid., 131–34.

[39] "Turkey Run is Now State Park," *Indianapolis News*, 11 November 1916. See also, Richard Lieber, "Report of Park Committee," *The Indiana Centennial*, 53; Frederick, "Colonel Richard Lieber," 134; and Hoy, "Samuel M. Ralston: Progressive Governor," 205. In discussing the park committee's victory, the *Rockville Tribune* noted that people in Parke County had claimed all along that the Hoosier Veneer Company wanted the Turkey Run tract not for the trees on the property, but to give the firm "an outlet for hauling logs a shorter route, these logs to be brought across the creek [Sugar Creek] and 'snaked' up the hill at the camping grounds, saving a haul of several

miles around the upper road." See, "Turkey Run a State Park," *Rockville Tribune*, 14 November 1916.

[40] See, Department of Conservation, *Turkey Run State Park*, 15; Phillips, *Indiana in Transition*, 221; and *Laws of the State of Indiana* (Fort Wayne Printing Company, Contractors for State Printing and Binding, 1917), 221.

[41] Phillips, *Indiana in Transition*, 222–23.

[42] Department of Conservation, *Turkey Run State Park*, 41–42.

Chapter Six
THE WOMAN WHO WEARS THE HALO

Even before Strauss had embarked on her attempt to persuade Governor Ralston to preserve Turkey Run, the Rockville native had become well known to the rest of the state and the nation, not only through her written work done for the *Indianapolis News* and *Ladies' Home Journal*, but also through her ability as a speaker. Her talks before Hoosier audiences caught the attention of the Affiliated Lyceum Bureaus, which signed her on as a lecturer. In the fall of 1917 and the winter of 1918, the Bureau—a nationwide lecture service with offices in Cleveland, Boston, Pittsburgh, Chicago, Atlanta, Dallas, Boise, and Portland—sent Strauss on a lecture tour to communities in the south, east, and west. She took as the subject for these talks, "How Mother Got Her Halo."[1] According to a promotional pamphlet distributed at her stops, Strauss's lecture was based upon the idea of "bringing the beauty and light of spiritual things to the doings of the difficult and common tasks of every day." The Country Contributor believes, the pamphlet continued, that the "brightest halo" surrounding any human face adorns that of the old-fashioned mother "who meets the affairs of life in the cheerful, uncomplaining way peculiar to people who have learned the great lesson of 'finding themselves' in their native element." Also at her lectures, Strauss discussed questions that were of "public interest," particularly how these questions related to women and to the home.[2]

Strauss's success on the lecture circuit came during the heyday of the Chautauqua movement, which had been established in the 1870s with the Chautauqua Assembly at Lake Chautauqua, New York. Lecture bureaus like the Affiliated Lyceum organized "traveling chautauquas" featuring educational talks combined with enter-tainment usually performed outdoors in tents. In 1911, Rockville started its own Chautauqua association. Held at Beechwood Park, the Rockville Chautauqua over the years drew crowds as large as eight thousand people to hear such nationally known speakers as Rever-end W. A. "Billy" Sunday, William Jennings Bryan, Elbert Hubbard, and William Howard Taft.[3] Strauss's secretary, Skelton, said that the Chautauqua lecture circuit "proved intensely interesting and satis-fying to her [Strauss]." Strauss brought to this task the same determi-nation and dedication she showed in her writing, Skelton noted. "I saw her start out in the teeth of our great blizzard last winter [1917] to fill her engagements," said Skelton, "when it was difficult to get strong men to venture forth, but there was no thought so far as she was concerned save that the lecture should be given on [its] schedule[d] time."[4]

Her growing fame as a writer and lecturer did not, at least in Strauss's mind, translate into acceptance in her own hometown. While people from all over the country wrote her letters telling her how much they admired her work and asking The Country Contribu-tor to address their clubs, farmers' institutes, and Chautauqua asso-ciations, "people at home were ignoring me," said Strauss. Although she was often invited to neighboring communities to meet other "celebrities," Strauss told her *Ladies' Home Journal* readers, she was "studiously omitted" when a Rockville club brought celebrities to town. "I have often addressed all sorts of audiences . . . with what is termed great success," she complained, but the only recognition she ever received from the Rockville Chautauqua association was to be asked to preside over an afternoon session at a woman's day from which all the males "promptly absented themselves." (She refused the honor.) Real or imagined, such snubs hurt Strauss deeply. Instead of putting on a brave face as she had in the past, she admitted her pain: "If you imagine this did not deeply and sorely wound me you have little real understanding of a woman's heart," she said. "I suf-fered all the loneliness and longing which any woman who sees her neighbors having a good time without her suffers."[5] It would take her death for her Rockville neighbors to finally realize Strauss's worth.

Strauss's busy schedule, as her friend Riley had feared, took a toll on her health. Sometime in late winter or early spring of 1918, Strauss, who had just returned from a lecture tour, checked into the Culver Union Hospital in Crawfordsville for surgery to help relieve her suffering from ulcers. Brought back home to Grouch Place, it seemed at first as though Strauss might recover. Late in May, however, The Country Contributor, aged fifty-five, fell into a coma and, in spite of blood transfusions, died at six o'clock in the evening on 22 May 1918. On Strauss's death certificate, her Rockville physician, Dr. Raymond E. Swope, listed as the cause of death "Progressive Pernicious Anemia" (a deficiency in the oxygen-carrying component of the blood), along with "Chronic Nephritis" (inflammation of the kidneys) as a secondary cause.[6]

Even after death, Strauss lived on through her writing. Always taking pride in her ability to never miss deadlines, Strauss had, from time to time, prepared a number of "emergency"columns in case, for whatever reason, she was unable to produce her regular weekly department. "Promptness in her work was her pride," Skelton said of her employer. "Whatever happened her work must go on as usual."[7] In memorializing its former columnist, the *Indianapolis News* noted that a week before Strauss's death her secretary Skelton wrote the newspaper "asking whether one of these articles, written a number of months ago, was not on hand and requesting that it be sent for revision." In spite of her ill health, Strauss managed to revise the column, titled "In Defense of Exaggeration," and return it to the *Indianapolis News* where it ran in its regular place in the newspaper's Saturday edition on 25 May 1918.[8] This last column, begun by Strauss with pen and finished with pencil, said Skelton, was written "under stress of so much pain that it was difficult for her to collect her thoughts, but under conviction that her duty must be well performed she pushed on, completing an article, somewhat short, but well rounded nevertheless."[9]

Strauss showed the same dedication toward her work for the *Ladies' Home Journal*. For seven months after her death, her "The Ideas of a Plain Country Woman" column appeared in its regular spot in the magazine. Her final piece, which warned against spreading rumors and idle gossip during wartime, included a picture of Strauss and a statement from the *Journal's* editors about her death. Noting her foresightedness in providing extra manuscripts, the editors noted that they and the magazine's readers would "miss her as a wise counselor, a kindly philosopher: we who knew her will miss her not only as such, but as a woman and friend." No writer in the magazine's history, the editors added, have ever "come so close to our readers as did 'The Country Contributor.'" Although regretting her passage, the magazine's editors noted they were grateful that for "so many years it was our privilege to give her helpful messages to so large a public."[10]

Strauss frequently believed she had been misunderstood by her community, and subjected to criticism that, her husband's newspaper the *Rockville Tribune* noted, was "a hard trial for one so sensitive, and whose motive was always a desire to do good for the town she loved so well," but Rockville showed great respect for Strauss upon her death.[11] At her funeral service, held at Rockville's Memorial Presbyterian Church on Saturday, 25 May 1918, long before the scheduled start "the church was well filled and when the exercise began every seat as well as many chairs in the aisles were occupied," reported the *Rockville Republican*. The town's businesses also closed their doors in Strauss's honor during her funeral. As her coffin, which had been escorted by an honor guard from the First Indiana Infantry, entered the church, the organist played "The Pilgrim's Chorus," one of Strauss's favorite songs. In his eulogy, Reverend W. R. Graham praised Strauss for her capacity at winning the love of her friends, the charm and power of her personality, and her gift of expression. "All over this land, and into far away lands," Graham said, "in thousands of homes, 'The Country Contributor' is a household friend. It is safe to say that no woman of her time in this country has found a place in the hearts of so many others of her own sex." Tributes to Strauss included a telegram of condolence from Bok, her *Journal* editor; a poem in her honor by George Bicknell of the Affiliated Lyceum Bureaus; and an obituary sketch written by a girlhood friend. Strauss's body was interred in the Rockville Cemetery next to her beloved daughter Sarah Katherine.[12]

Accolades for Strauss's life and work poured in from all over the state. In a special memorial supplement, which quickly sold out, Strouse's *Rockville Tribune* included editorial tributes from newspapers in Terre Haute, Fort Wayne, New Castle, Muncie, Greencastle, Princeton, and Indianapolis. Her employer, the *Indianapolis News*, said that in Strauss's weekly essays could be found a "very sound and helpful philosophy. One can read in them a love of simplicity and genuineness, an earnest and honest faith, a hatred of sham and pretense, and a belief in the home and family as the great educators."[13] In its tribute, titled "Our Best Known Citizen," the *Rockville Republican* said the strength and appealing quality of Strauss's writing were due to her ability to take "the commoner things of the plain simple life of a people not sated with over-indulgence, not tired to death with 'nothing to do,' and discussing these in a bright, sparkling style." She pointed out to her readers the "foolishness of many common faults, habits and customs and indicated the way to a better, broader and more satisfying manner of living." No other Rockville citizen, the newspaper said, ever "met more noted people of our land than she and no other Rockville citizen ever gained a position of honor so high as she among the noted writers of the Hoosier state and this is a large company of notables."[14]

In addition to the printed tributes, a more permanent memorial to Strauss's life came a few years later. Shortly after her death, fellow *Indianapolis News* writer Herschell penned a final farewell to his friend. In writing about her life, Herschell noted that it was Strauss who first proposed that Turkey Run be bought by the state and preserved for future generations to enjoy. For his story, Herschell talked with another person who had been a major force in saving Turkey Run: Lieber. Recently returned from a trip to Turkey Run, Lieber told

Herschell that Indiana "owed Mrs. Strauss a great debt." To help repay that debt, Lieber said that some "fitting memorial, marking her devotion to the cause of state parks, should be placed in Turkey Run." The conservationist suggested that a log cabin, then being built at the park above Rocky Hollow, should be used as the memorial to Strauss, complete with a bronze plaque in her honor. "It is the hope of Mr. Lieber," Herschell said, "that the women of Indiana, particularly, will approve his suggestion and move to honor one of their sex who has done so much for humanity."[15]

Lieber's call for a memorial to Strauss at Turkey Run drew immediate attention from one group, the Woman's Press Club of Indiana. The club, founded on 18 February 1913 and dedicated to providing "a means of communication between women writers," believed it was especially fitting that it be the organization to honor Strauss as it was the only club The Country Contributor had ever joined (Strauss had been one of the club's twenty-eight charter members).[16] On 11 June 1918 the club, during a luncheon at the home of Mrs. Samuel M. Ralston, voted unanimously to erect a memorial to Strauss at the state park and appointed a committee to plan such a site. At the meeting, club members suggested several ideas for a memorial, including a bronze seat or a sundial surrounded by an old-fashioned garden.[17] "We were all so grateful that Turkey Run had been saved from the timber interests," said Susan McWhirter Ostrom, Woman's Press Club recording secretary, "and felt Mrs. Strauss should be memorialized for her leadership in creating public sentiment for this state park to be saved."[18]

Embarking on a campaign to raise money for the memorial from the public, the Press Club committee found that the "money filtered in slowly," according to Blanche Foster Boruff of Bedford, who served as the committee's chairman. During the fund-raising campaign, which lasted for four years, the committee received letters with contributions from every state in the country, as well as from Canada, England, and Australia. "They [the letters] all told of the wonderful help and inspiration they had received in reading the 'Ideas of a Plain

Country Woman' in the Ladies' Home Journal," said Boruff, who noted she volunteered her services for the memorial campaign because of her "keen love and admiration for Mrs. Strauss."[19]

The Press Club selected Myra Reynolds Richards, an Indianapolis sculptress, to design the Strauss Memorial, which she titled *Subjugation*. The state's first memorial ever to be erected to honor a woman was unveiled at Turkey Run with an impressive ceremony on the afternoon of Sunday, 2 July 1922. In spite of rainy weather, approximately four thousand people, including most of Strauss's surviving family, gathered at the park for the memorial's unveiling near Turkey Run Inn. As part of the ceremonies, Boruff read a letter from Bok, who could not attend the event, but who expressed his fondness for Strauss "as a woman, aside from our relationship as contributor and editor. She was a constant delight to me, and always an inspiration." Unveiled by Strauss's granddaughter, Juliet Ott, the statue stood eleven feet high perched atop a circular base etched with the words: "In Memoriam, Juliet V. Strauss, The Country Contributor, By the Woman's Press Club of Indiana."

The work featured the graceful figure of a woman holding a goblet aloft and, after its unveiling, water slowly trickled from the goblet. Richards explained that the statue is "symbolical of woman's triumph over the baser things; innocence holding aloft the goblet of purity; at her feet the crouching figures of the lion, symbolizing force; the tiger, ferocity; young boar, gluttony; and peeping from the folds of the robe, an ape suggesting the false or mimicry, while one hand rests upon the head of a peacock back of the figure."

In May 1938, due to problems with piping water to the statue, park officials moved the memorial from the inn to a new location along the west wall of a sheer cliff at Turkey Run Hollow on Trail Number Six.[20] Fifty-eight years later, the Strauss statue was moved again as part of ceremonies to mark the eightieth anniversary of the founding of Indiana's state parks. The *Subjugation* statue was reconditioned and moved from its Trail Six location to a site near the Turkey Run Inn. Rededication ceremonies for the memorial to Strauss were held on 26 October 1996.[21.]

Today, the statue erected in Strauss's memory is one of the few tangible pieces of evidence left about her life. Her husband, long-time *Rockville Tribune* editor and owner Isaac Strouse, who retired from the newspaper business in May 1924, died at Grouch Place on 5 December 1934. Marcia Strouse Ott, the couple's surviving daughter, kept the family's journalistic tradition alive by becoming a columnist for the *Rockville Republican*. Ott's column, "Talking It Over," appeared on the front page of the weekly Parke County newspaper from 1957 until her death on 17 July 1974 at age ninety-one. For her final column, a "popular and well-read weekly feature," the newspaper noted, the *Rockville Republican* paid tribute to Ott by placing the journalistic notation,—30—, signifying the end of the story, at the top of the piece.[22] As for the family home, Grouch Place, it still stands in Rockville, now used as a bed and breakfast establishment known as "Suits Us."

Unlike those of her Hoosier contemporaries—Riley, Tarkington, Nicholson, Ade, and Stratton-Porter—Strauss's literary contributions to the state's history, which share the same sentimental flavors as those by more well known authors, have faded from the scene. Strauss's devotion to the idea of women being best suited for life in the home seems reactionary and outdated from today's perspective. In her countless writings for newspapers and magazines can be found, however, ideas that still resonate for modern readers: not following fashion's dicates, being true to oneself, and the worth of those who take care of home and family. Strauss not only advised her readers to find beauty and spirituality in their own lives, but she fought to protect it in her own life through her successful effort to preserve Turkey Run's grandeur. In her own time Strauss's words were read and appreciated by countless numbers of readers. Housewives across the country gained strength from Strauss's work and her belief that being a "plain home woman" was one of the greatest successes in life. While some might have viewed such work as drudgery and the person performing it as common, Strauss believed that a woman who worked with her hands year after year in the house and kitchen, reared a "creditable family and still kept for her soul a pair of wings like a dove, is the perfect flower of civilization."[23]

Notes

[1] "Death and Funeral. Of Mrs. Isaac R. Strouse, the Well Known 'Country Contributor,'" *Rockville Republican*, 29 May 1918.

[2] *Mrs. Juliet V. Strauss, The Country Contributor of the* Ladies' Home Journal (*Rockville Tribune*, n.d.).

[3] Strouse, "The Rockville Chautauqua," *Parke County Centennial Memorial*, 126–27.

[4] Skelton, "Mrs. Strauss at Work," *Rockville Tribune Memorial Supplement*, 4 June 1918.

[5] The Country Contributor, "The Ideas of a Plain Country Woman," *Ladies' Home Journal*, January 1917.

[6] See, "Death and Funeral," *Rockville Republican*, 29 May 1918; "Juliet V. Strauss Dead at Rockville," *Indianapolis News*, 23 May 1918; "Juliet V. Strauss. Dies at Her Home in Rockville on Wednesday Evening After an Illness of Only a Few Weeks," *Rockville Tribune*, 28 May 1918; and "Juliet Strauss Expires at Her Rockville Home," *Indianapolis Star*, 23 May 1918.

[7] Skelton, "Mrs. Strauss at Work," *Rockville Tribune Memorial Supplement*, 4 June 1918.

[8] "Juliet V. Strauss Dead at Rockville," *Indianapolis News*, 23 May 1918.

[9] Skelton, "Mrs. Strauss at Work," *Rockville Tribune Memorial Supplement*, 4 June 1918.

[10] The Country Contributor, "The Ideas of a Plain Country Woman," *Ladies' Home Journal*, December 1918.

[11] "Reminiscence," *Rockville Tribune Memorial Supplement*, 4 June 1918.

[12] See, "Death and Funeral of Mrs. Isaac R. Strouse, the Well Known 'Country Contributor,'" *Rockville Republican*, 29 May 1918; "Juliet V. Strauss," *Rockville Tribune*, 28 May 1918; and "Funeral Discourse Delivered by Rev. R. W. Graham Saturday Morning," *Rockville Tribune*, 4 June 1918.

[13] "Juliet V. Strauss," *Indianapolis News*, 23 May 1918.

[14] "Our Best Known Citizen," *Rockville Republican*, 29 May 1918.

[15] Herschell, "State Park Head Urges Memorial to Juliet V. Strauss at Turkey Run," *Indianapolis News*, 1 June 1918.

[16] See, Woman's Press Club of Indiana yearbook, 1913, Woman's Press

Club of Indiana Papers, Indiana Historical Society, Indianapolis.

[17] "Memorial at Turkey Run for Mrs. Juliet V. Strauss," *Rockville Tribune*, 18 June 1918.

[18] Wayne Guthrie, "Spirit of Strauss Fountain Sought," *Indianapolis News*, 30 August 1974.

[19] "Juliet V. Strauss Memorial Fountain," *Rockville Tribune*, 5 July 1922.

[20] See, "The Strauss Memorial. Beautiful Fountain Unveiled at Turkey Run Last Sunday," *Rockville Republican*, 5 July 1922; "Juliet V. Strauss Memorial Fountain," *Rockville Tribune*, 5 July 1922; "Strauss Memorial at Turkey Run Unveiled," *Indianapolis News*, 3 July 1922; and Guthrie, "Spirit of Strauss Fountain Sought," *Indianapolis News*, 30 August 1974.

[21] "Rededication of Memorial Tops State Park Celebration," *Parke County Sentinel*, 23 October 1996.

[22] See, "Isaac R. Strouse, Former Tribune Editor, Succumbs," *Rockville Tribune*, 5 December 1934; Miller, *Indiana Newspaper Bibliography*, 353; "M. O.—Local Columnist Dies July 17," *Rockville Republican*, 22 July 1974; and Wayne Guthrie, "Columnist Knew Death Was Near," *Indianapolis News*, 1 November 1974.

[23] Strauss, *The Ideas of a Plain Country Woman*, 20.

Appendix 1

The following is an early piece of fiction Strauss wrote. The story, "A Secret of the Hills," was discovered in 1920 in an old desk at the In-dianapolis Journal *by a longtime employee of that newspaper. Apparently mislaid and never before published, the manuscript eventually made its way to the* Indianapolis News, *which published the piece on 12 June 1920. The newspaper noted that the story features an aged woman of the South leading a lonely life (her family had been wiped out in the Civil War) in a mountainous part of Virginia.*

"A Secret of the Hills"

The silence had been so oppressive around my old stone house that day I know I was glad when the thunder began to roll and tumble over the north mountain.

I mind it was in harvest time and the men came galloping in from the fields with the gears clattering about the horses and the light-ning spitting at their heels, for all the world like the flash of gun-powder.

I had no fears of the hurricane myself, and I liked the break in the day's monotony. Silence was not always the portion of my life. In my young days there were music and laughter and happy voices, the patter of dancing feet, the clatter of saddle horses and the roll of car-riages and all of the varied sounds that make up the measure of that harmony to which is set the lives of the fortunate.

Even after I wedded with my sober sided husband and came here to live with him in the fastness of this rocky valley there was life and bustle enough, and I was happy, though many thought it a strange choice, and indeed I wonder at it myself, though perhaps it was his very gravity, so unlike the gay sparks of our part of the country, which won my fancy.

We were not many years man and wife before the war came on and then came the great silence and I was alone in the old stone house. Father, brothers and husband all went down and I remained, though many a time I wished I, too, might have fallen beside them. My husband's slaves remained about me and I made shift to live, and by and by I found a certain interest in the business of the farm and as the black men were faithful, my affairs prospered, and so the years passed by. I knew little of the people around me. Their ways and mine were ever different and changes came, removing from the neighborhood even the few that I had known. I was busy all the day, for I had a dairy and a garden and small apiary and many things to occupy my mind, and it was only at twilight that I was wont to feel my loneliness and I had a fashion of standing in my doorway peering up and down the road with a "feeling" that somebody might be coming, though none ever came, for I was esteemed a queer old woman by the ignorant youngsters of the neighborhood and the older ones whom my husband had known (good, sober people, they were) were either dead or too infirm for visiting.

However, as I stood that evening watching the hurrying men and the strange wind-ridden twilight, I saw a carriage scuddling before the blast, and before I could think to wonder who might be traveling this lonely road at this time of day, the driver drew rein at my own door and the inmates of the vehicle sprang out and ran laughing and gasping on to my veranda just as the storm broke in an avalanche of heavy drops.

In the tumult of the storm and the surprise of their sudden appearance, I had much to do to receive them properly, but I brought them inside and gave them such welcome as I could at the time command.

The two strangers who had thus unexpectedly laid claim upon my hospitality were a man and woman of surpassing grace and beauty. Not since the days of my girlhood had I met any persons with just the bearing, the appearance and the gentle speech of these two belated travelers. In their soft voices, their musical laughter, the texture of their clothing, the daintiness of the woman's ensemble and the courtliness of the man's address, I seemed to feel myself borne into the past, and could almost have fancied that the stormy twilight had blown me two ghosts from the long ago of my own life.

They had not gained the shelter of my old house a moment too soon, for no such storm ever before broke over the valley, as raged for hours that night. In the midst of it all, however, I made shift to entertain them as best I could. I changed my gown to one of gray silk which my dear husband had made for me at Richmond just before the war, and I altered the appearance of the supper table which the black woman had laid for me as usual by placing upon it my best linen, which indeed I had never used in this part of the country, and by placing upon it a service of silver and china which had long been hidden from the light of day. I also lit the candles in the candelabra and gave out an extra white apron and a better turban for Susan, who was all agog with delight at the presence of visitors.

I gathered that the lady and gentleman were traveling to Washington, and, attracted by the wonderful beauty of our valley had left the railway, and were traveling by carriage to a point further east where they might again resume their journey by rail. The gratification of such a whim bespoke unlimited means and leisure, besides a goodly appreciation of the lavish beauties of nature. I perceived right well that they found me quaint and interesting, and it was little wonder that I seemed so in their eyes, since I had learned little and forgotten nothing for nearly forty years.

Their amusement, however, had in it no flavor of ridicule; rather, it was tinged with a reverent tenderness grateful enough to me, who had sometimes felt myself the object of the buffoonery of the ignorant young farming people about me. It was years since I had met with people out of my own world and I was glad enough to converse with them and to show them many of my little treasures and note their quick appreciation of the things, the value of which I alone had known for many years.

The rain kept falling heavily and I prevailed upon my visitors to remain with me all night, though they were for going forward to the village, where there was a tavern or boarding house, little fitted, I thought, for the accommodation of such guests.

I can not say but that I enjoyed preparing for their entertainment; lighting a little blaze upon the hearth to drive away the dampness from the great chamber, and laying out my best linen for the bed. I doubted not they were a newly wedded pair, for I noted how his eyes followed her about and thought I saw upon her face at times a wistful questioning which is natural enough on the face of a bride, but which I feared was more pronounced than I wished to see on one so beautiful as hers.

I lay awake a long time that night for such a happening in my quiet life was like to drive sleep away, and besides I was busy with plans for breakfast and for sending Susan up the hill bright and early for blackberries to give a relish to our plain fare.

I fell into a doze, however, after so long a time but was presently awakened by a strange sound which, upon sitting up in bed, I made out to be that of a woman weeping.

A woman weeping at dead of night was a sound not wholly unknown to the old house, for there had been times when grief lay heavy on my heart, and I had no wish to yield to weakness in the daytime when the servants eyes were upon me. But as I listened to this desperate, yet subdued weeping, sounding so strangely in the silent house, it came to me somehow that I had never wept like that, or even heard any woman weep so in all my life before.

Susan was sleeping soundly on her pallet beside my bed, and I stole quietly to the window and looked out. The storm had subsided and the rain died quite away, and the moon was shining dimly through a veil of thin white cloud. By its light I perceived a woman, my guest of the night, I made no doubt, crouched down in an old arm chair which had stood for years upon the upper veranda. Being sleepless she had risen and, as the guest chamber opened on the veranda, she had found her way out there.

Never before had I felt upon my heart such heaviness as her weeping laid there, and there was, in her whole attitude such an abandon of wretchedness and despair that I shuddered as I looked, and wondered what I might do for her. As I stood in uncertainty, I heard the door swing gently and saw my other guest, partially dressed, step out upon the veranda. He stood for a moment looking down upon the woman, and then he spoke to her. I had thought the night before that his speech was the most musical, courteous and fascinating I had ever heard from man's lips. Now, though his tones were modulated as those of a gentleman, and his language graced with its wonted polish, there was in his voice something that chilled the blood—a dry, sarcastic cadence tempered with an affected patience and a deadly ennui unlike anything I had ever heard before and fraught with a suggestion more insolent, more stinging than any number of harsh or bitter words.

"This is very fatiguing, Louise," he said. "You are entirely exhausting yourself and robbing one of a night's rest. If you have soon changed your mind upon a matter so important; if you have so easily worn out your love for me, do not lay the blame at my door. Remember, you are a woman not a child. Look matters in the face. Is anything gained by such hysterical demonstrations?" He paused for a reply, but as she made none he proceeded: "As you evidently wish it, we will abandon the idea of a trip abroad. I will arrange for your comfort wherever you wish, or if you can do so, return you to your mother—"

A low moan broke from the woman. "Oh, my God," she murmured, not wildly, but with a set despair more terrible than frenzy. "Oh, my mother! Oh, my baby—my little, little baby!"

"Perhaps," said the man, and I saw upon this handsome face a sneer of cool contempt, "perhaps if you should return, your husband, even if he failed to forgive you, might at least allow you to have your child."

The woman suddenly sat erect. She pushed her heavy hair from her face and looked the man squarely in the eyes. "You forget," she said very quietly, "that my husband is a gentleman; he can never forgive one so dishonored as I, and he would never for one moment consider allowing me even to see the child that I have deserted. As for my mother, she is already dead. No one has told me, but my heart knows it. Return to your bed," she added with a gesture of command. "I shall not disturb you again. I shall do very well here until morning."

The man's face softened at her reply and drawing closer to her he fell upon his knees by her side and gathered her into his arms. I could hear him whispering to her. Soon her head sank upon his shoulder, but I could see her profile, pale and set in the moonlight, and catch a gleam from her eyes, open and staring like those of the dead.

Trembling and sick at heart I sank down on the floor of my chamber. Here then I was in the presence of a deadly sorrow and a deadlier sin! With two of earth's vilest sinners under my roof! And here was that most abhorred creature, a lost woman, come to me in a form so beautiful that I had loved her and fairly longed to clasp my lonesome old arms around her.

And then it suddenly came to me that, though by her own confession I knew how great had been her sin, I still had it in my heart to love her. I still longed to go to her and lay her pretty head upon my own bosom.

Indeed I could have wept when I recalled the tone in which I had heard her say, "My mother! my baby!" and I knelt up suddenly from the floor where I was lying and asked the good God to help her and tell me what to do. Yet the only guidance I received when morning had at last dawned, was to send Susan for the blackberries and lay out breakfast and pack up a basket of luncheon for the travelers, just as I had planned the night before.

My guests, when they came down to breakfast, seemed very much themselves again. The woman was pale and I noted the carefully concealed traces of her heavy weeping, but the speech of both was as gracious and their bearing as charming as I had found it when they came so unexpectedly into my house from the storm. But a few moments before their departure I came on the woman standing alone on the veranda, gazing back over the road the two had traveled the night before. I went to her side and words were given me to speak to her. I placed my arm about her shoulders, and, drawing her to me, I said, "My daughter,"—I thought she started at the word—"when you find yourself in strange places remember this old quiet house. When unfriendly faces are about you, think then of this queer old woman with whom you stayed the night. If life can not be borne in your new environment and you are seeking a place to go, return here, where there is peace, and I will receive you, for my heart goes out to love you as if you were my own child."

I looked long and earnestly into her face and she returned my look, with one as long, as earnest and as full of meaning. She understood me, and no more words passed between us before they drove away.

————

My mind was much disturbed for many weeks after this strange event. I felt continually that more was to follow, and sent Susan to the post office oftener than she cared to go, but no letter came and never a token to remind me of that strange night.

By and by I thought less about it, but I seemed suddenly to have grown more lonely, the house more desolate, and deep in the night I would wake from troubled dreams and fancy that I heard a sound of woman's weeping.

As months passed away I sometimes found myself half believing the thing itself a dream were it not for Susan breaking in upon my fancy with one of her harangues upon the beauty of that strange young master and missus who stopped in out of the storm and the grandeur of the young missus's gown and flashing of the rings upon her fingers.

It was a seasonable year, I mind me and autumn tarried late so that it was November before the first fires were lighted and the leaves began to come down to showers about the old house.

At last came a chilly day, and the wind at twilight blew dolefully over the hills and sighed about the great chimneys. According to my custom I walked out to the gate as the dusk gathered. It was a fancy of my own to stand there and, in a dreaming mood, half look for those who could not come again, yet who it sometimes seemed must be coming. How often I had waited here for my dear husband's return on a market day, or for the welcome sound of wheels, when my father and mother were expected from over the mountain! Tonight the sense of some loved one coming home was strong upon me—and as I looked, behold a single foot passenger came wearily down the hill, a slender woman in a black gown; the wind pushing her rudely and scattering the brown leaves all about her.

Her face was wan and her eyes were hollow, but in spite of the change since I had seen her last, I knew her, and I stepped out into the road to meet her. She had remembered—and she had come back.

When I led her into the house, I knew that I admitted with her a guest before whose majesty the kings of all the earth must bow. For death had left his imprint on her face and she bore about her the dignity of his royal insignia.

I laid her down on my bed, and drew the blankets close and warm about her, and Susan and I waited on her for many days. I never saw her weeping, and once or twice she smiled as I sat and held her hand. And once I whispered to her, "Had you not better tell me your name, and where was your home, beloved?" But no, she only shook her head and answered, "It is better so."

Well, then I thought that I was done with strange happenings in my quiet life and so it was until two years later, once more a carriage drew rein at my door and a traveler alighted. He was a young man in years, no doubt, but the hair on his temples was white as snow and his shoulders, which I fancied had once been erect and square, drooped as if some weight of grief or shame had come prematurely upon them. He asked me if a woman had died at my house, and by his description I knew whom he was in quest of. I saw that he was a man to be trusted, so I told him all the story just as I have told it to you.

He listened in silence and when I had done, he asked me to show him her grave. How long he stood beside it with bared head I do not know. I came away and left him there. When he returned, he told me that he had come to take away the body to a new resting place, beside her mother, he said, and where her little girl might go and visit the grave. Then he thanked me again and again for what I had done, and the next day he took her away.

He was a fine, quiet gentleman, but as I looked at him and heard him speak, I knew that, while his heart was true and his life above reproach, he was lacking in that lordly charm and brilliancy which had distinguished another whose name and history I have never known.

Well, this is the end of the story, and all that remains to remind me is a tiny marble slab which I have left standing where her body used to lie and upon which, in compliance with a whispered request of her own, made in the still twilight of one of those mild winter days during which I watched beside her, I had engraved in the rude lettering of our country stonecutter:

"I was a stranger and ye took me in."

Appendix 2

The following is Strauss's first column as The Country Contributor *for the* Indianapolis News. *The column, "The Short and Simple Annals of the Poor," appeared in the newspaper on 21 November 1903.*

"The Short and Simple Annals of the Poor"

I realize the fact that, though youth is far enough behind me, I am still too young to indulge so much in retrospect. Retrospect is for the chimney corner, with knitting and patchwork, and one ought really to save it up with this in view and go on making history until the last moment, so that the stores of reminiscence may be full to repletion. Perhaps then, when the evil days do come, the household will not tire so dreadfully of our repertory. If one did not repeat the same story oftener than, say, once in six months, or such a matter, one might hope to hold an audience among the juvenile members of the family for some years. However, the retrospective habit grows upon me, and with it a tendency to philosophy and reflection really dangerous to a woman who still wears gay colors and tries to wear her hair in pompadour.

In one of my philosophie moods the other day I fell to wondering what in the world the poet (Gray, was it not?) meant by speaking of the short and simple annals of the poor. If there is anything in the world that is eventful it is being poor! Poverty figures in novels and romances almost as largely as love. And I do believe the dearest stories in all the world are about poor people. Where would be the charm in "Little Women" if the March family had been rich, or who would have cared half so much for Jane Eyre if she had not wandered out penniless and alone and had not nearly died of "starvation and sorrow"? I am desperately fond of an impecunious heroine. I want her to look prettier in her skimpy gray gown and white gull's feathers than the black-eyed heiress in her velvet and sables. But truth compels me to state that I have a sneaking fancy for the hero with a fair backing of filthy lucre, or at least a rich uncle in the background, who dies in the nick of time. I am sentimental to a degree, but I want a financial basis of some sort. It is very uncomfortable for me to see a hero and heroine launched on the ocean of life with only love for their guiding star. No doubt my own experience has shown me how good a thing a little of the dross of riches might be, even for those who think they care only for love.

However, Mr. Gray to the contrary, I insist that the annals of the poor are anything but short and simple, and are on the other hand fraught with excitement, exigencies, makeshifts, romances and little tragedies of which the rich, the stupid rich, know nothing. I am glad that my memory goes back to old-fashioned village scenes, to times when we lived close to life and primitive things, and nature was very near to us, and we never went very far from the beginning of things. As we grow older the charm of simplicity grows upon us. We wish to put away the complications of our lives and to get back once more to a sense of nearness to mother earth—dear mother earth, who told us all we know and in whose rugged bosom we shall sleep at last.

In the old days we lived a religious life. The church was much to us. Sunday was the jewel of the week: our workday world was toned and modulated by spiritual emotions and teachings. My father died when I was a tiny girl and it was my mother's idea to bring us up in the nurture and admonition of the Lord. To this end every function of the household arrangement was turned, and the mere suggestion that we were not in special charge of divine authority would have been received as rank heresy. I was an arrant little pagan from the start, given to cat-napping through thirdlies and fourthlies, and to bringing my elders up short with unanswerable questions deemed perfectly scandalous by my aunts, but forgiven in secret by my mother, who in moments of loving communion admitted that there were many things one could not explain, but must just take on faith. We took so much on faith in those days that I surely should not repudiate it now, and I would not, only that it does seem we also owe a good deal to the staying qualities of the old Franklin stove, the three-ply carpet and the silver spoons that were great-grandmother's.

We had great pretensions to gentility. We had good blood in us, but I have seen the time, sitting in the sanctuary, looking ruefully at my copper-toed shoes and inwardly loathing my "waterproof" cloak, that I really cared as little for good blood as I did for faith, heartily wishing myself rid of both, like the little girl who sat behind me, resplendent in pretty and fashionable garments, kid shoes and a hat with a feather in it! In vain my mother told me the little girl was "common"; that she lived in a rented house and her mother used bad grammar. I wished to live in a rented house. I was tired of our house with its queer little windows, it bleak white front door and the garden hugging it quite up to the back porch. Some people had iron fences; ours was a high, white "picket" affair, with rather unsteady gate posts, and I resented the fact that the weight in the chain which pulled the gate shut was a jug—just a stone jug—when some people had stylish weights to their chains, made on purpose. The fact was there were many things we had which were not "made on purpose," but which would "do."

Meanwhile, our "annals" continued to be exciting. There was always some crisis at hand. The daily business of eating and drinking, over which my mother and aunt had personal supervision, was interspersed with problems of consuming interest. There was invariably a quilt in the frames or a carpet in the loom, or there was a garden making, or apple-butter stirring, or hog killing. In lieu of these stirring events there was the never-ending problem of wherewithal shall ye be clothed. Miracles of evolving something out of nothing were being constantly worked, and the result was an aggressive gentility, which, being a little pagan, as aforesaid, I cordially hated. In the midst of all this strenuous, happy life, we found time for mild social occasions. Inviting the minister's family for tea was a yearly ceremony, and there were also neighbors and visiting dignitaries to be entertained at stated intervals. The discipline of children in those days was a thing to make the devils believe and tremble. I could be relied on to misbehave and get a whipping after the company was gone, so I really dreaded the social aspect of our lives as much as the genteel phases.

The presence of chicken and jelly in the cut-glass dish usually sobered me to some extent, but the dreadful threats as to what would be done to us if we should laugh or speak at the table so worked upon our sensibilities that we invariably gave way from sheer nervousness and laughed out, leaving the company to speculate as to whether it was the preacher's whiskers, which had a funny way of wagging up and down when he ate, or our uncle's peculiar method of "making an eye" at us to enforce discipline, that had started us going.

There was a little, shiny, brown teapot that was a great comfort to me at such times. It reflected my face in all sorts of queer distortions, and, oddly enough, this had a tranquilizing influence upon me, the only difficulty being that when I tried the effect of twisting my face up to see how it would look, I was invariably accused at the bar of justice, to which I was brought later, of having made faces at my aunt, who sat behind the teapot—a perfect pillar of gentility, with her best fringed cape and white apron, and her hair puffed at each side of her head into what we children irreverently called "horns."

In spite of the drawbacks incident to the original sin of childhood, I liked these social occasions. There was a sense of opulence in having a fire in the parlor and spare bedroom, and one could afford to swagger a little out on the sidewalk when he met other children whose mothers were cutting carpet rags when ours was giving a tea party. Every dog has his day.

I do not remember just where it was that the church slipped out of my life and prayer-meeting was no longer an event of the week, but I fear it was about the time that certain young gentlemen began dropping in, in time for the last hymn or hanging about the doors with a crooked arm and a half whispered "May I see you home?" Be that as it may, there were many years in which as a family we filed down the aisle to the third pew from the front every Wednesday evening for prayer-meeting. And here again the question of discipline was a vexing one. My sister and I between us had almost enough sense of humor to have made a man of us. You may believe this when I tell you that we invariably found fun in a Wednesday evening prayer-meeting. There was an old lady who pulled at her husband's coat tail when he talked too long. Our uncle had a habit of going to sleep, making it necessary to poke him when called upon to lead in prayer, and once our aunt went to this same Wednesday evening service with her bonnet on hind side in front. In later years I have seen bonnets and hats that really looked quite as rational one way as another, but this was a sincere, open-faced bonnet and the wayfaring man could tell at a glance when it was not properly adjusted. We made the discovery after we were seated and the hymn had been given out. It was "Coronation" and pitched rather high so the little shrieks of laughter my sister and I gave were drowned in the shouts of "And Crown Him!" that went up as my aunt, having discovered the mistake, calmly took off the misplaced head gear and turned it around. This time we were not punished for laughing in meeting. There is a limit even to discipline and our mother was mindful of us and remembered that we were dust.

When I think how my own children were allowed to take part in the conversation, laugh at nothing, run and tear over the house and speak at all times, whether spoken to or not, and see how much better they are than I ever was, I think that in my day children were little martyrs. I remember that my sister remained under a dark cloud of family displeasure for an entire summer because she told her grandmother that she ran like a cow. I suffered for her because of the snubs she got after her unlucky speech, and did all I could to alleviate her disgraced position. I even went so far as to confide in her that no matter how unpopular her comparison of her grandparent's means of locomotion to those of a cow might be among grown folk, I thought she did run like one, and so did our little sister and our cousins, and that moreover, grandma was an "old thing." I am a little ashamed of this now, in view of the fact that my grandmother was an uncommonly bright woman, but if she had only known enough to laugh at what my sister said, instead of going on her dignity over it, the effect upon the child would have been infinitely better.

———

I believe that the popular idea of happiness is to be able to live in luxury. I have never tried it, but I feel somehow that it would be irksome. There must be more zest in living the closer one gets to the rudiments of life. We hear women complain of dullness and see them searching through the days and years for something of real interest to fill their hearts and atone for the things of which civilization has robbed them. The gentle village women whom I knew in my childhood had no such anxieties. There was no time for ennui, and I believe there was fineness and quality in their lives that is woefully lacking in the lives of women today. Nothing is more undignified and underbred than restlessness and discontent—and I think with regret of the placidity of the lives of those women of a past generation. How smoothly the work went on and how sweet were those homely industries, followed without a thought of regret or any sense of injustice in having to follow them.

I remember many queer implements perfectly familiar to my childhood, which would not be recognized by half the grown people to-day. Carding machines and candle molds, quilting frames and steel-yards, snuffers and sand boxes, reel and spindles and lead ladles and bullet molds!

One family in our neighborhood enjoyed the distinction of owning a "grabhook." The uses of the well were more varied than they are to-day. Nearly all wells were open with windlasses of some sort for drawing water and low curbs, which were a standing invitation to children and little boys like Johnny Green of Mother Goose fame, who were seized with a desire to play a serious practical joke on the family cat. The well was commonly used as a refrigerator, milk, butter, eggs, custards and all sorts of things being suspended into the cool depths on hot summer days. The frequency of accidents called the grabhook into requisition so often that it was regarded as common property and barefoot youngsters were apt to dodge in at the kitchen door with such requests as, "Say, Mrs. _____, will you let me have the grabhook? Our bucket's gone to the bottom?" Or, "Can I get the grabhook? Ma's butter fell in the well."

———————

I often wonder how in a day's time all the work was done, but I recollect that it was a wonderfully cheerful way of living. There was much sunshine in it. I can see it now filtering through the grape arbor and making little checkers through the hop vines on the back porch, where somebody was ironing and the churn dasher was thumping, another was sewing, one child cleaning and decorating the bird cage, while the others were playing or helping with bits of work destined to be part of their education in later years.

Yes, there is much sunshine in these short and simple annals of the poor! Our poverty, however, was not of the worst sort. We were poor only in worldly goods and gear. Our spiritual and intellectual endowment was very fair. There is no poverty like narrowness of mind and soul, but we had treasures that moth and rust could not corrupt. Poetry, history, books of travel and romance made bright the homes of winter evenings. Discussions of questions in philosophy, theology and national politics hastened the hours of toil. We were not unhappy people.

It is a doctrine of mine that the quality of mind does not change with what we call civilization, except for the worse. In luxury the mind deteriorates, while simple and primitive living lightens it. It is good fortune to be born in a quiet country place close to fields and water and real work, and the woods and animals, the trees and clouds and weather—and all sorts of teachers. Money and society and colleges and even travel have little to teach in comparison with life. Be careful then, how you classify the lives of the poor as paltry, or say of a friend who has known the storm and stress of poverty, "It is a pity." Never pity anybody who can say of his youth, "There was much of sunshine in it." Beware also of choosing the member of the family who has "got to be worth something" as the successful man. Success in life is a personal matter—it is the individual life that counts. Our modern civilization is the worst enemy to the individual life. There is too much herding together. Eating has become largely a spiritless and mechanical affair. Food which is prepared by other than loving hands loses the essence of soul nourishment that was an element of mother's cooking in the old village days when we were so happy and so poor.

Deliver me from people who take their pleasure in material things. Life has so many better things to offer that the greatest pity of all seems to me to be for people who care most for hats and gowns, chairs and rugs and all the soulless things made by man. Nothing is quite so common as style. Nothing so tiresome as mere etiquette, nothing so nauseating as the round of stupid gatherings we call society, and nothing so execrable as what women like to call "culture." Men never use this atrocious word. They could not do it and look each other in the face. The very intimation that a woman is "cultured" is enough to cause me to take to the woods in terror lest I should hear her do "stunts" of modulation with her voice and see her fix her painted and "preserved" face into smirks of cultured toleration for my crudeness. I make no special crusade against "cultured" men (there are no cultured men—when they become hopelessly cultured they are all the same sex), but I do resent their claim upon being "the real thing." Just now in our shifting and unstable civilization there is little enough of the real thing. Our society is chaotic, because classes are not definitely assigned. Nothing is more fatally sure than for a people who are seeking a real democracy to become divided into two great classes, the rich and the poor. If birth does not count (though we all know in our souls that it is the only thing that does count) money is certain to become the criterion. Meanwhile, people who care for "a few friends and many books" must content themselves with such unwritten laws of natural selection as their environment permits, and for the rest cultivate selfishness with might and main.

If we are going to admit it, which we are not, life comes pretty near to being a tragedy at best. Only homes and quiet days of sweet renunciation and tremulous hope, only the family and the fireside, the love of man and woman held together by children of that love can save it from being so. Only great nature, with her wonderful variety, her philosophy and promise, her insistent religion, her reiteration of God before law, can fortify us for the trials of life and its final apparent defeat. All of these are the special blessings of the poor, and he only is really poor who fails to use them. I am so devoted to my village, with its sweet simplicity, its quiet intelligence, its near friendships, and its general "hominess," that nothing could draw me away from it save the promise of a still simpler life in a really "new" country, where brains and muscle and physical strength and courage are the things that count. But I should be lost there now. One goes to a new country while he still has youth, and I forget very often that mine is gone. I am a girl until I look in the glass or hear some young person place me with the middle-aged people, or take thought how long ago things happened, and remember that my lengthy and brilliant annals of the poor transpired far back in a past century.

Appendix 3

The following are two Juliet Strauss columns taken from the collection of her work The Ideas of a Plain Country Woman, *originally published in the United States and Great Britain in 1908. Strauss used "The Woman Who Wears the Halo" column as the basis for her many lecture appearances.*

"The Woman Who Wears the Halo"

Being a plain country woman, born and reared in a little inland town, I lived a good many years of my life before it occurred to me to speak out in meeting and say a few words that might reflect the daily reveries of thousands of women situated as I am, and reassure them a little as to the purpose of their being, which seems at times to be called into question by leaders of the woman movement. There are plenty of hard-headed, sensible women who know that the woman movement is a delusion, and who have the hardihood to smile indulgently when the woman lecturer comes telling us what is the matter with us, and to get up the next morning and take up the business of life in perfect peace of mind, undisturbed by the suggestion that women ought to be looking after higher things.

There is nothing the matter with the most of us aside from the natural afflictions that flesh is heir to, and most of the aspirations that women are struggling with are fool notions promulgated by somebody who hasn't anything better to do.

I heartily dislike the idea of there being a "woman question," but suppose if there is one it hinges upon woman suffrage. I get dreadfully tired of the reiteration of the suffragists and the persistent division between men and women that they themselves make by constantly seeking to bring women into prominence. I hate references to what women are doing. It would be so much better simply to say "what people are doing." The very stress upon the matter of sex implies that it is a miraculous thing for a woman to do anything. Women prove themselves to be in the infancy of their mental development by calling attention to the capers they cut, and particularly so because in no branch of art or industry has woman, as a class, proved herself the equal of man.

Though our list of notable women is a long one, the fact remains that the great geniuses of the world have been men. This should not be especially discouraging to women. The world doesn't need many geniuses. If you ever lived in the house with one you would be convinced that a little of him goes a long way, and after he was gone, and the family happily back into the old rut of being nobody in particular and having a good time, you would count your many blessings in a very tranquil state of mind.

Woman attained her highest glory centuries ago, and the brightest halo that is worn by a face in our galaxy of saints and immortals is won not by a distinction of genius or of valor—though the woman who wears it has both—but rather by the simple carrying out of a manifest destiny, a brave and cheerful acceptance of the existing order of things.

I am not much of a reformer, being doubtful of the real good of many things that we call progress, but I am not going to set myself in the path and get run over by them. One can keep out of their way and besides, although there is a lot of fuss over the changing conditions of woman's lot and the new régime, when the shouting and the tumult die it will be seen that there is a respectable minority living close to the ground, holding to the old ideals, and, above all, minding their own business—which is genius of the highest order.

I am not much of a suffragist, either, if the truth must be told, possibly because I have always had so many more rights than I knew what to do with. There are already so many more things than one can attend to that it seems to me if I had the franchise and should suddenly find some added duties of citizenship thrust upon me it would be the last straw.

There has never been any let or hindrance to my life. I am free to fire the furnace, shovel the snow out of the paths, hoe in the garden, dig potatoes, whitewash the back fence, trim the grapevines, curry the horse, or engage in any other manly occupation I choose. If the burglar gets in the house I can get up and shoot him if I want to. If I take a notion to go anywhere I can get on the train, take my own money, pay the hotel bill, and stay as long as I please.

My husband believes in woman suffrage. He is willing, even anxious, for me to vote. He runs a Democratic newspaper in a strongly Republican county, and he often needs my vote and wishes he had it. I have no doubt if we had woman suffrage he would see that I got to the polls. He always sends our horse and buggy out to the poor-farm for the few paupers who remain staunch in the face of Republican prosperity, and, as they have to pass our house, no doubt would stop for me on the return trip. The only condition would be: if I had the time to go. And then I feel sure I should worry all night under the impression that I had made a mistake in some way and not stamped the rooster! [symbol for the Democratic party] I am not very methodical. Personally, I shouldn't mind this uncertainty, but my husband knows the poll of our precinct to a vote, and if there were one out of pocket I am sure he would lay it on me and accuse me of doing it on purpose. I haven't any political convictions whatever, and it would be a lot of trouble to have to acquire them at my time of life.

I am a great hand for living a day at a time, and I presume this is the reason I haven't many convictions. A day isn't long enough for them to form in, and by the next day there is always something else to do.

I do not know whether this is the best way to live, but it has its advantages. In looking back it seems as if there were a lot of days—and that is a good thing! A long string of days, each with its complete story, is like a rosary of fragrant sandalwood.

I remember days better than years, and some of the days seem the longer—no doubt they are. Our little chronology may not count for much in the great reckoning, but supposing there should be a day or an hour in our brief span that was worthy of being noted in the calendar of Eternity? How then? The day belongs especially to the women. Men think in years and the decades, but woman's life is in the details of the big scheme of things, and she sometimes rebels that it is so, and wishes that she, too, might take a hand in epoch-making.

I have said to you that I haven't many settled convictions, and this is true; but I do have leanings toward certain doctrines, and among them is the idea of reincarnation—that is, of our coming back again and again to try it all over until we learn. Surely the women who have never had to work are not worth saving until they have been tried by the fire of daily toil.

Some years ago there came a rumor, trailing over the country, as the folk-songs travel on the gossamer threads, that there was something new for woman. It unsettled us all a little. I was young and easily unsettled, and I felt a strong desire to go in for higher things, but fortunately never got the chance. I did go to cooking school, though, and learned how to serve things in bits of millinery and how to work over scraps of things we so seldom had at home that there was never a scrap left. I came home one November afternoon and began telling mother about some new recipes I had learned. She listened and finally asked: "Did she give you a recipe for pulling turnips? That is what I have been doing all afternoon." I thought it a little sarcastic of mother to say this, but have since looked at it in a different light. The turnips had to be pulled you know, because it was going to freeze that night.

My mother was not a new woman, but I am quite sure she had the proper theory of life. You never went into her kitchen but you found there a copy of some entertaining or instructive book. You never helped her wash the dishes without learning something widely removed from dishes. Hers was the secret of a most successful way of living, and it is a way that any thinking woman can adopt. She could not go out into the world, but she could bring the world to her.

Wherever you are, wherever there is a point of alert, interested consciousness, there is the center of the universe. To be interested is to be happy, and to be happy is simply to be in accord with your world. A sense of this truth may come to you anywhere—over the washtub, out in the garden where the early corn is rustling, in the poultry-yard when you hear the sleepy chirp of a little chick under its mother's wing. If you have suddenly felt yourself thus in touch with the Universal, know that it is a revelation, but do not be in a hurry to tell about it.

The way to do things is to do them, and the way to be somebody is just to be it.

There is never any glory in trying to do something which you cannot do, but there is always great honor and credit in doing anything well. Being a plain home woman is one of the greatest successes in life, if to plainness you add kindness, tolerance, and interest, real interest in simple things.

There is a text of Scripture that applies particularly to women, and I think of it when I see one of our village women with a delicate ivory-tinted face and snow-white hair—"Though ye have lien among the pots, yet shall ye be as the wings of a dove"—and I smile when I see how intrinsic is that spirit of womanliness that rises white and unsmirched from life's scullery and its seeming degradations, and I wonder why it is that we are called upon to see and know all the unspeakable side of life, to bear the burden of it—do the menial tasks, hustle out of sight the debris, the ghastly accumulations of daily living, and make the face of life sweet and attractive for man, for coarse, sinful, unsympathetic man, who is big and strong, yet who cannot bear the sight of such things! Then, after wondering a bit I come back to the old doctrine that service is the crowning glory of life, and that through it alone do we lay hold upon the eternal; and then I cease to wonder how mother gets her halo—I know, and I know, too, that it is none too bright and glorious for the service by which she earns it. Every woman is a mother at heart, but it takes a mother in fact to know things just as they are.

When I am feeling quite well, and my joints and muscles sing with the joy of living, I am glad to the heart that God put me in the industrial school of life and allowed me to take in its lessons at my finger tips. But when I am sick, and the physical machinery runs heavily, I fret a good deal, and feel envious of those women who have never had to learn the real lesson of life.

I think no great lady with her knowledge of the world, her fine philosophies, and her education, can tell a bright, sensible woman who has borne children and has done her own housework anything really worth hearing about woman's life. I believe no preacher with his hands soft from idleness can instruct her, and I feel sure that no layman with a reasonable share of mother-wit would attempt it. When it comes to arriving at the point she has the right-of-way, and if she rules the house and makes the entire family walk a chalk-line it is no more than she ought to do! The intelligent woman who has done real work—and by real work I mean labor with her own hands year after year in her own house and kitchen—and who has meanwhile reared a creditable family and still kept for her soul a pair of wings like a dove, is the perfect flower of civilization, far superior to the woman of the world who knows the lingo of polite society and little else.

The people who count in this world are those who, if everybody else were suddenly stripped of every worldly possession, cast upon a desert shore, and confronted with only the raw material for living, would know how to take hold of it.

I was telling a woman who was visiting me of my preparations for a dinner, and how I went out early in the morning of the day before and killed the turkey. She held up her hands in horror.

"My dear, you didn't kill it yourself?"

"Yes, I killed it, and it was a twenty-pound gobbler and came pretty near to killing me!"

"But how could you kill it?" she said. "I couldn't kill a chicken if my life depended on it."

I looked at her speculatively, and I declare I believe it was true. I don't believe she could kill one. I think she would just daintily curl up and die first.

"Why, Mrs. Blank," I said, "if my children were hungry, and there wasn't anyone else to do it, I could go out myself and kill a cow!"

I don't like to kill things; in fact, I hate to, but I can if I must. And this makes me think of a little episode in my life. I have been accused of having psychic powers, but really I am not so gifted, though I have had some peculiar experiences in having dreams come true and seeing things that are not strictly in the landscape.

One Saturday morning, several years ago, I got up with the feeling of being at the end of the rope. I don't know how often I have been at the end of it—a good many times, I suppose—but nobody would ever help me let go. This morning, however, I felt I simply must let go. I was sick and tired and discouraged. I felt that it was too bad for me to be ploughing around the kitchen at work when the sun was shining, and lots of people were out riding in parks, and sailing for Europe, and doing all of the beautiful things I was quite as well fitted to enjoy, but never would do.

After I got the dishes washed, and the bread made up, and a cake baked, and the porches scrubbed, I remembered about two chickens I had put under a tub the night before to be dressed for Sunday. There was just about time to wring their necks and dress them and get them safely on the ice before I started in to get dinner. But I was seized with a violent attack of the dreadful "I don't want to's." I went into the library and lay down on the lounge, just flattened out. I said to myself that I didn't care if the chickens smothered under that tub—the sun was getting dreadfully hot by this time—nor if the children didn't have any fried chicken for Sunday dinner. I didn't care for anything—I was at the end of the rope!

My mother used to have a way of taking down the Bible, opening at random and reading the seventh verse. She said it invariably gave you a clue to the solution of your difficulties. There was a big, old-fashioned dog-eared Testament on the table just within reach of my hand. I took it listlessly, opened it, ran my eye down to verse seven of the eleventh chapter of the Acts, which I happened upon, and read the words: "And I heard a voice saying unto me, Arise, Peter: slay and eat." (At home I have the reputation of telling yarns, and they pretend not to believe me when I recount anything marvelous. But I don't tell yarns. Truth is stranger than fiction, and this actually happened just as I have told it.)

When I read the verse I broke out laughing. And when you are downhearted a laugh is the only thing that will cure you. I felt better instantly, got up, and went out and slew the fowls, and got through the day in good shape.

It is not easy to laugh when one is tired, and really I am afraid my sisters are a little lacking in a sense of humor. I wish when Adam gave up that rib he had also parted with some of the funny-bone, so that his help-mate might be able to see the joke oftener. It would be a good deal of use to her when the clothes-line breaks or when the cow kicks the bucket over.

We can't help holding a little grudge against life for making us do the little, menial, hateful things that women must do, and my knowledge of the fact that those who can do them and still be sweet and fine are the chosen ones doesn't help me in certain moods. I think rebelliously that I would rather not be a chosen one, but be allowed to slip along easily, neither learning nor developing.

I know quite well how it is with many people who have the things I think I long for. I know that the people who run away from winter and summer, impiously "making their own climate," are running away from life. They are loosening the blessed moorings of home and gaining only the curse of the roving foot. I know that people who can buy fruit out of season are purchasing satiety and spoiling their taste for the simple and sweet products of the earth as they come to us according to Nature's plan. I know that the rich have no treasures. Nothing excites them with a sense of novelty. The little purchase, the little journey, the little glimpses of society that seems a wonder to me means nothing to them. They have tried everything; and people must be interested, so they fall back upon immoralities, pitifully seeking for new sensations. Now, I do not mean that all rich women do this, for many rich women have sense enough to live above wealth, just as the rest of us live above poverty; but this state of affairs exists in very "high" society, and the reason for it is apparent.

A woman may know all this and still in moments of despondency half wish that she, too, might live the idle, irresponsible life of flowers and light and music and perfume.

In thinking of men and women it is difficult to select from the male sex a type of the ideal man, but the heart leaps instantly in homage to the feet of the woman who wears the halo, and is to wear it, please God, till the end of time. I think it will always be an old-fashioned face, a little worn with time and toil, a little touched with sorrow, a little lacking in that hard, manly knowledge one sees in the faces of woman-suffrage speakers. Woman's lot will change with the changing times, but the conditions for wearing the halo will remain the same. Women may attain a certain freedom of action, but there will be no more freedom of mind. Mind is always free. We have been told that the book, the picture, the piece of music must, if it is to be called true art, be of a great simplicity, that the wayfaring man can understand. So this face that wears the halo must be written in lines that every human being can read. It must not show too many of the refinements of life, or much pride of culture or learning. It must be a rugged face, warmly touched with tenderness, lightly brushed with ladyhood to endear it to the truly refined, but with no affectations nor superfluous elegancies to frighten the timid or repel the humble.

"Philosophies of a Housecleaning Day"

I like to "talk about cats and things" and think it no disgrace to exchange recipes and discuss housekeeping methods, but the "smart" woman of modern times has looked with contempt upon such common conversation—thinking we should discuss more vital topics. This is surely from misapprehension of the word—she must have forgotten what "vital statistics" are.

I wish I knew what it is they want, these women who constantly express in such impassioned strain their discontent with life, but more, I wish that they themselves knew. Only the suffragists state it definitely. They want equal rights with man. I am not an anti-suffragist or anti anything else—I am merely setting down impressions as they come to me uninfluenced by much that affects the trend of thought of most women writers, but it is impossible for me to believe that the franchise would do other than complicate the "woman question." The Civil War did not solve the "Negro" problem.

But then, I only know how the franchise would affect me. If an angel with a flaming sword should appear before me this minute and say, "You are free, you may vote, you are a citizen," it would not change one feature of my life. I should have to get up and get breakfast in the morning and go on with my housecleaning just the same.

That I had an even chance with man in the business world would not bring me business ability. My arms would not be stronger to strike with the hammer nor my legs more sturdy to follow the plough. I should still be subject to every limitation of sex.

The business woman who complains to me that women are not paid well for their work would not have her craft more at her fingertips for equal rights.

The majority of women do not know what it means to work as men work, steadily, moment by moment. They drudge, and allow a sense of bodily degradation in doing it to pull them down and break their spirit, but they do not in the least understand what physical and mental force must be expanded in the mastery of a trade or a profession. Very few women are fit for this concentrated application. It is not a "fair chance" that women need to make them the equals of man in this sense; it is bone and sinew and reserve force in brain and nerve cells.

Not that woman is a sickly creature, or even a weak one, but is not "built" to be man's rival in the business or professional world. I believe this with all my heart, and also I believe that she is peculiarly fitted for the varied activities of plain home life.

As to the injustice of our laws as they pertain to the personal and property rights of women, here again I am at sea. When it comes to a woman's standing on her legal rights as opposed to her husband, or to squabbling over the children born of their union, the worst has already happened, and there is scarcely a dignified way of settling the trouble.

I like to believe that most people are sane and healthful in spirit, and I shrink from the details of domestic infelicity which loose divorce laws encourage, sensational newspapers promulgate, and careless moral sentiment is responsible for. Women talk too much of these things. If men talked more we might have a revelation as to what many of them have to endure from sordid wives who insist on being "kept" like lilies of the field, who refuse to rear families, and rebel against the responsibilities of housekeeping.

While I sympathise deeply with the trials of my sex and know that many of us bear them nobly, I am convinced that women are often unreasonable in their demands upon men's time, patience, love, and pocketbook. I know it is an accepted idea that men have everything their own way; that they slight and neglect their wives, and that women are powerless to retaliate. But much of this is exaggerated by women's morbid brains.

Women are fed on morbid mental diet almost from the cradle. Fiction, which women and girls read omnivorously, is largely morbid. Religion as dispensed by sentimentalists is morbid. We are fairly swamped in morbid health-fads, and women let their minds run on imaginary ills, accepting the ridiculous idea that we are a race of invalids. The truth is, Nature takes good care of the mothers of her race, and, when not interfered with, she manages finely. I hope we may hear less complaining, less abominable testimony, less damaging admission of wrong living, and that women will get back to the normal and to the eternal truth that can never be changed by an agitation of popular sentiment, will get over the idea that there will come a time when men will "understand"; it is woman who needs to understand.

Woman achieves her nearest equality with man when she is simply and healthfully alive and at work in her natural sphere, when she is not striving for recognition or whining for appreciation. "The king is but a man as I am—the violet smells to him as it does to me!" So, man is but a creature who lives and loves and dies. He breathes with pleasure the fresh air of the early spring, drinks clear water, smells the upturned sod, knows the delight of sleep and the taste of bread— am I not the same? But I am more. God has atoned to me for all the weakness of my nature; He has given me fulfillment where man has ever but an exquisite longing. He has given me the child, the warm nearness of its little head upon my heart, the blessed weight of its body in my arms. It is this human nearness, this mutual feeling for life, that makes man and woman one and obliterates all questions of equality, and in this simplicity of being we deeply sense the existence of purpose in all that we do and bear.

We country people are especially blessed with this nearness. Life is simple and its duties are plain, yet many of us do not know that this is a blessing. We look away to the city and sigh for its luxury and elegance, not realizing that we are the people who live close to the great secret which the world so often "stands tiptoe to explain."

Did you ever try being happy just because it was raining or snowing or blowing, or because it was April or May or November? Any of these is sufficient reason for being happy, but few people know it. Indeed, young people are discouraged by ambitious parents and teachers from yielding to moods of being happy over nothing, and counseled to strive and grasp and attain and accumulate, forgetting everything but the work in hand. Men in hot, dusty offices and stores and counting-rooms must indeed do this, but women, more blessed in their work at home, may keep close around them a sense of what the beautiful world is doing, and share in the impressionistic rapture with which April clothes the faintly greening woods with dandelions and streaks the color on startled tulip petals scarcely awake and aware.

I used to have a friend come from the city to visit me. She would sit in the kitchen while I worked and lament over my hard lot, and the fact that I was buried in this little backwoods town. "Youth and beauty are so precious, and talent so rare," she used to say. "It is an outrage for yours to be sacrificed working for a man and children." She would often get me worked up into such a state of self-pity I wonder I did not commit some dreadful folly, for I was young and had not yet learned the deep meanings of life. But she was wrong in every premise. Youth and beauty are not precious, neither is talent rare. The years are merciless to us all, and I think, the "well-preserved" woman of forty with her massaged face and juvenile costume looks her years more painfully than the sweet country mother with life's dear story written on her strong, quiet face.

My friend was a good woman and her sympathy was genuine, but she did not know what she wished for me and had nothing to offer me but the pernicious seed of discontent. Do not allow what people of this sort tell you of the glories of the "outside world" to distress you. There is no outside world. Life is life, and the world is your world.

The woman who is cleaning house on an April day is so fatally prone to allow her happiness to depend upon other people and upon circumstances judged by other people's standards. This is a little way of looking at life. Suppose your house is old and plain and its furnishings shabby as compared with your neighbor's. Does not April love you just as well—is not her face quite as tremulously tender, do not her robins sing their world-old love song at twilight, and is it not for you?

Step out into the April night some time when you are perplexed by life's problems, and see the stars hanging down from the sky. Feel the fresh tides of the year throbbing, half-hear the stirrings of sprouting things and the nestlings of young creatures to sleep and mother. Imbibe the trust in which they go to rest, and take the gift which life is constantly offering you. If you ask me what that gift is I reply that it is a soul quickened with a willingness to live and trained to the proud humility of obedience which takes rank with command.

In trying to tell women of a serenity that may come into their lives if they will only admit it, I do not mean that they can arrive at a point where everything will move so smoothly that there will be no friction. Too many impractical writers have told women this. It is easy to put on paper a plan for smooth, perfect action in the home and kitchen. But we who have lived there year in and year out know better. We know that the dishes will not wash themselves while we go out to drop corn or plant potatoes or sow early garden seeds. The little garment we left on the sewing-machine when we got up to cook dinner will be there when we return, and if the bread runs over the pan while we are out making a bed for sweet peas it will be too light and have big holes in it—or if we "work it down" it may taste sour when it rises again. I believe the thing which most frets the woman in the kitchen is the idea that many of her sisters live without care and worry while she must degrade herself with toil. If this were true we should still be the fortunate ones; but it is a great mistake. Life does not move without effort for any really bright people; friction keeps us alive, and the woman whom you see idly sitting around is a dull person whom you should not envy.

One great cause of the unrest among women is the idleness enforced upon many of them by riches. They take up foolish, baseless causes just to have something to do. I visited a rich woman not long ago and watched her lounging about in the morning while an overworked maid was hurrying through the rooms striving to get things straightened up. My fingers fairly itched to help her, and I saw so much the mistress of the house might have done with pleasure and profit to herself and her digestion, and with great benefit to her home and relief to the harassed maid.

Perhaps what these women who write to me of longings and ambitions unsatisfied need to do is to cultivate appreciation. Whatever we really appreciate is ours. It is a possession nobody can take from us. We need to look at life in the abstract as a thing of wonder and beauty.

We must learn to regard suffering and trial through the sublimity of what they bring with them: courage, patience, endurance. We must learn to see death through the beauty of renunciation, classic as the marbles and cypress trees that typify it.

As for happiness, it, too, is symbolical. It belongs to us exactly in proportion to our appreciation of it. People who know what happiness is are happy. Only those who do not understand remain fretting like foolish children.

I am persuaded that much of woman's "unquietness" comes from wrong thinking about marriage. I look with much disfavor on our modern hesitation over the "advisability" of marriage. This foolish and immoral attitude is part of the "woman question"—and woman is responsible for it. Middle-aged women who think they are "sensible" constantly remind young women to look ahead and see what the man can give them of "the good things of life." This coarse expression embraces the cut-glass, sterling silver, finery of all sorts, uselessly shod feet, fine white hands and general elegance which young women are taught they must have. This attitude on the part of womankind, more than any other thing, is responsible for Old-World immoralities which are said to be growing in our great cities with shocking rapidity.

I am glad that I live out in the big world of spring, where I can see the farmers breaking ground and feel the deep religion of such vital work. Men go daily into avenues of money-making with a sense of dishonesty in their hearts, but the ploughman can never doubt he is doing "God's service" when he plants the seed for bread.

I am glad to work in the exquisite light of the April morning—

glad when a dainty little shower comes lilting across the meadows, driving us all in from our planting, and pelting the bowed heads of the tulips and jonquils—glad when the thunder rolls along the distant hills and the sun flashes out again and life and the day's work are before me.

SELECT BIBLIOGRAPHY

General References

Arnold, Eleanor, ed. *Voices of American Homemakers*, Bloomington and Indianapolis: Indiana University Press, 1985.

____. *Feeding Our Families: Memories of Hoosier Homemakers*, Indianapolis: Indiana Extension Homemakers Association, 1983.

____. *Party Lines, Pumps and Privies: Memories of Hoosier Homemakers*, Indianapolis: Indiana Extension Homemakers Association, 1984.

Beasley, Maurine H. and Shelia J. Gibbons, *Taking Their Place: A Documentary History of Women and Journalism*. Washington, D.C.: American University Press in cooperation with the Women's Institute for Freedom of the Press, 1933.

Beckwith, H. W. *History of Vigo and Parke Counties, Together with Historic Notes on the Wabash Valley*. Chicago: H.H. Hill and N. Iddings, Publishers, 1880.

Beecher, Catharine E., and Harriet Beecher Stowe. *The American Woman's Home or, Principles of Domestic Science; Being a Guide to the Formation and Maintenance of Economical, Healthful, Beautiful and Christian Homes*. 1869. Reprint, Hartford, Conn.: The Stowe-Day Foundation, 1994.

Bodenhamer, David J. and Robert G. Barrows, eds. *The Encyclopedia of Indianapolis*. Bloomington and Indianapolis: Indiana University Press, 1994.

Bok, Edward W. *The Americanization of Edward Bok*. 1920. Reprint, Philadelphia: Consolidated/Drake Press, 1973.

____. *A Man from Maine*. New York: Charles Scribner's Sons, 1923.

Brown, Hilton U. *A Book of Memories*. Indianapolis: Butler University, 1951.

Carmony, Donald F., ed. *Indiana: A Self-Appraisal*. Bloomington: Indiana University Press, 1966.

The Country Contributor [Juliet V. Strauss]. *The Ideas of a Plain Country Woman*. New York: Doubleday, Page & Company, 1908.

Damon-Moore, Helen. *Magazines for Millions: Gender and Commerce in the* Ladies' Home Journal *and the* Saturday Evening Post, *1880–1910*. Albany, N.Y.: State University of New York Press, 1994.

Dunn, Jacob Piatt Jr. *Greater Indianapolis: The History, the Industries, the Institutions, and the People of a City of Homes*. Vol. 1. Chicago: The Lewis Publishing Company, 1910.

____. *Indiana and Indianans*. Vol. 2. Chicago: The American Historical Society, 1919.

Evans, Sarah M. *Born for Liberty: A History of Women in America*. New York: The Free Press, 1989.

Filler, Lewis. *The Muckrakers*. 1939. Reprint, Stanford, Calif.: Stanford University Press, 1993.

Flexner, Eleanor, and Ellen Fitzpatrick. *Century of Struggle: The Woman's Rights Movement in the United States*. 1959. Reprint, Cambridge, Mass.: The Belknap Press of Harvard University Press, 1996.

Hawes, David S., ed. *The Best of Kin Hubbard: Abe Martin's Sayings and Wisecracks, Abe's Neighbors, His Almanack, Comic Drawings*. Bloomington: Indiana University Press, 1984.

Hoy, Suellen M. *Chasing Dirt: The American Pursuit of Cleanliness*. New York: Oxford University Press, 1995.

Kelly, Fred C. *The Life and Times of Kin Hubbard, Creator of Abe Martin*. New York: Farrar, Straus, and Young, 1952.

Langdon, William Chauncy. *The Pageant of Indiana: The Development of the State as a Community from its Exploration by LaSalle to the Centennial of its Admission to the Union*. Indianapolis: The Hollenbeck Press, 1916.

Lieber, Emma. *Richard Lieber*. Indianapolis: n.p., 1947.

Lieber, Richard. *America's Natural Wealth: A Story of the Use and Abuse of Our Resources*. New York: Harper & Brothers Publishers, 1942.

Lindley, Harlow, ed. *The Indiana Centennial, 1916: A Record of the Celebration of the One Hundredth Anniversary of Indiana's Admission to Statehood*. Indianapolis: Indiana Historical Commission, 1919.

Madison, James H. *The Indiana Way: A State History*. Bloomington and Indianapolis: Indiana University Press and Indiana Historical Society, 1986.

Martin, John Bartlow. *Indiana: An Interpretation*. 1947. Reprint, Bloomington and Indianapolis: Indiana University Press, 1992.

Miller, John. *Indiana Newspaper Bibliography*. Indianapolis: Indiana Historical Society, 1982.

Morrow, Barbara Olenyik. *From Ben-Hur to Sister Carrie: Remembering the Lives and Works of Five Indiana Authors*. Indianapolis: Guild Press of Indiana, 1995.

Mott, Frank Luther. *American Journalism, A History: 1690–1960*. New York: The MacMillan Company, 1962.

Nicholson, Meredith, *The Hoosiers*. New York: The MacMillan Company, 1916.

Owen County Indiana: A History. Spencer, Ind.: Owen County Historical and Genealogical Society, 1994.

Parker, Benjamin S. and Enose B. Heiney, eds. *A Representative Collection of the Poetry of Indiana during the First Hundred Years of Its History as Territory and State, 1800 to 1900*. New York: Silver Burdett and Company, 1900.

Phillips, Clifton J. *Indiana in Transition: The Emergence of an Industrial Commonwealth, 1880–1920*. Indianapolis: Indiana Historical Bureau and Indiana Historical Society, 1968.

Riley, Glenda. *Inventing the American Woman: An Inclusive History, Volume 2, Since 1877*. Wheeling, Ill.: Harlan Davidson, Inc., 1995.

Ruegamer, Lana. *A History of the Indiana Historical Society, 1830–1980*. Indianapolis: Indiana Historical Society, 1980.

Schneider, Carl, and Dorothy Schneider,. *American Women in the Progressive Era, 1900–1920.* 1993. Reprint, New York: Anchor Books, 1994.

Shumaker, Arthur W. *A History of Indiana Literature: With Emphasis on the Authors of Imaginative Works Who Commenced Writing Prior to World War II.* Indianapolis: Indiana Historical Bureau, 1962.

Steinberg, Salme Harju. *Reformer in the Marketplace: Edward W. Bok and* The Ladies' Home Journal. Baton Rouge: Louisiana State University Press, 1979.

Stewart, Kenneth, and John Tebbel. *Makers of Modern Journalism.* New York: Prentice-Hall, Inc., 1952.

Strasser, Susan. *Never Done: A History of American Housework.* New York: Pantheon Books,1982.

Strouse, Isaac. *Parke County Indiana Centennial Memorial.* Rockville, Ind.: Rockville Chautauqua Association, 1916.

Tebbel, John, and Mary Ellen Zuckerman. *The Magazine in America, 1741–1990.* New York: Oxford University Press, 1991.

Thornbrough, Emma Lou. *Indiana in the Civil War Era, 1850–1880.* Indianapolis: Indiana Historical Bureau and Indiana Historical Society, 1965.

Tredway, Gilbert R. *Democratic Opposition to the Lincoln Administration in Indiana.* Indianapolis: Indiana Historical Bureau, 1973.

Walsh, Justin E. *The Centennial History of the Indiana General Assembly, 1816–1978.* Indianapolis: The Select Committee on the Centennial History of the Indiana General Assembly, in cooperation with the Indiana Historical Bureau, 1978.

Weber, Ronald. *The Midwestern Ascendancy in American Writing.* Bloomington and Indianapolis: Indiana University Press, 1992.

Wiebe, Robert H. *The Search for Order, 1877–1920.* New York: Hill and Wang, 1967.

Woloch, Nancy. *Women and the American Experience.* New York: McGraw-Hill, Inc., 1994.

Wood, James Playsted. *The Curtis Magazines.* New York: The Ronald Press Company, 1971.

Articles

Bartholomew, H.S.K. "Newspaper Work at the Turn of the Century." *Indiana Magazine of History* 35 (September 1939).

Boomhower, Ray. "Celebrating Statehood: The Indiana Centennial of 1916." *Traces of Indiana and Midwestern History* 3 (Summer 1991).

____. "'Devoted to the Past for the Sake of the Present': George S. Cottman and the *Indiana Magazine of History*." *Indiana Magazine of History* 93 (March 1997).

Cottman, George S. "The Western Association of Writers: A Literary Reminiscence." *Indiana Magazine of History* 29 (September 1933).

Fesler, Mayo. "Secret Political Societies in the North during the Civil War." *Indiana Magazine of History* 14 (September 1918).

"Hoosier Conservationist: Juliet V. Strauss." *Outdoor Indiana* (May 1944).

Hoy, Suellen M. "Governor Samuel M. Ralston and Indiana's Centennial Celebration." *Indiana Magazine of History* 71 (September 1975).

Murphy, Maurice. "Some Features of the History of Parke County." *Indiana Magazine of History* 12 (June 1916).

Peckham, Howard. "What Made Hoosiers Write?" *American Heritage* 2 (Autumn 1950).

Sawyer, Harriet Adams. "The Western Association of Writers: Some Impressions Received at its Recent Convention Held at Dayton, Ohio." *The Chaperone* 8 (August 1892).

Schell, Ernest. "Edward Bok and the *Ladies' Home Journal*." *American History Illustrated* 16 (February 1982).

Shi, David. "Edward Bok and the Simple Life." *American Heritage* 36 (December 1984).

Silver, David M., ed. "Richard Lieber and Indiana's Forest Heritage." *Indiana Magazine of History* 67 (March 1971).

Simons, Richard. "Christening a Rock." *Indianapolis Star Magazine* (5 April 1953).

Pamphlets, Papers, and Miscellaneous Sources

Department of Conservation, State of Indiana. *McCormick's Creek Canyon State Park: A History and Description*. Indianapolis: William B. Burford, Contractor of State Printing and Binding, 1923.
___. *Turkey Run State Park: A History and Description*. Indianapolis: William B. Burford, Contractor for State Printing and Binding, 1919.
Frederick, Robert Allen. "Colonel Richard Lieber, Conservationist and Park Builder: The Indiana Years." Ph.D. diss., Indiana University, 1960.
Hoy, Suellen M. "Samuel M. Ralston: Progressive Governor, 1913–1917." Ph.D. diss., Indiana University, 1975.
Lieber, William Leo. "Colonel Richard Lieber and Turkey Run State Park." Lecture at Indiana Historical Society's 21st Annual Indiana History Workshop, 1971, Turkey Run State Park.
Snowden, Juliet. *Legends and Lore of Parke County*. N.p., 1967.

Manuscripts

George S. Cottman Papers, Indiana Division, Indiana State Library, Indianapolis.
Delavan Smith Papers, Indiana Historical Society, Indianapolis.
Indiana Forestry Association Papers, Lilly Library, Indiana University, Bloomington.
Samuel M. Ralston Papers, Indiana State Archives, Commission on Public Records, Indianapolis.
Samuel M. Ralston Papers, Lilly Library, Indiana University, Bloomington.
Snowden Family Papers, Indiana Historical Society, Indianapolis.
Woman's Press Club of Indiana Papers, Indiana Historical Society, Indianapolis.